La Verde de la Vida

Wisdom for the Abortion War:
A Peaceable Answer
Without Compromise

Shining River Press

Dedicated to the children of the world and my country.

America the Beautiful

O beautiful for spacious skies,
For amber waves of grain,
For purple mountain majesties
Above the fruited plain!

O beautiful for pilgrim feet
Whose stern impassion'd stress
A thoroughfare for freedom beat
Across the wilderness.

America! America!
God mend thine ev'ry flaw,
Confirm thy soul in self-control,
Thy liberty in law.

O beautiful for heroes prov'd
In liberating strife,
Who more than self their country loved,
And mercy more than life.

America! America!
May God thy gold refine
Till all success be nobleness,
And ev'ry gain divine.

O beautiful for patriot dream
That sees beyond the years
Thine alabaster cities gleam
Undimmed by human tears.

America! America!
God shed His grace on thee,
And crown thy good with brotherhood
From sea to shining sea.

Contents

La Verde de la Vida

Among the Trees of Van Cortlandt Park

I sit here on a bench among the trees of Van Cortlandt Park enjoying the rare November sun, grateful to feel its warmth on my face. I like to come to the edge of this urban forest to meditate, to pray and to write in my journal and watch as one season fades into another. Soon winter will be here and the last leaves will be gone. The days being shorter and the weather at times bitter, my visits will be fewer. Yet winter is not without splendor. I've noticed how the naked branches reveal their form and have their own beauty. How wonderful to walk when first snow falls and my tracks are the only ones in a clean, quiet world! And spring always comes. First the soft, fuzzy pussywillows, then the dancing branches of the yellow forsythia—from a distance

1

the little buds on the trees look like an impressionistic painting. In summer, the foliage, full and green, protects like a canopy. Summer wanes and the leaves crescendo in vibrant color. I've loved sitting on a carpet of golden leaves.

How many times, my thoughts scattered, with too many concerns overwhelming me, and tears in my heart, have I run to this refuge? With relief I sit on a bench and my cares miraculously fall away -- my mood lifts. I enter the place where Time Is. I love to sit here and let time stand still. Often, I sit motionless—like Robert Frost looking into the woods, lovely, dark and deep. . .

Even as I do now.

Knowing my days of coming here will soon be limited, I linger long. I think of my three children and seven grandchildren. I think of things happening in the world. I write thoughts, names, verses in my journal. As sun begins to set, I pick up pen and paper and walk towards the sunset and home, leaving the park behind. Before reaching my apartment, I cross a busy street with cars and buses and a crowded sidewalk. Can I keep the ambiance, the stillness with me midst all the noises of the street?

For some time I've been disturbed about the wrangling— yes, that word describes it. Everywhere this wrangling—on the left, the right, words jumping to judgment on the page, circling the globe on the Internet—truth distorted mixed with outright lies—words without knowledge—like undisciplined children. I am aghast at who is popular—who is becoming wealthy by polarizing, destroying with their tongues. And throngs of people following, like the pied piper, the most outrageous of voices. "At the heart of the wrangling. . .is the abortion issue." That's what the headlines of a newspaper articles repeatedly say and it's true.

"We're expected to have the wisdom of Solomon," said a legislator way back in 1990 regarding the boiling abortion issue. Apparently the wisdom of Solomon has not been forthcoming for we are still stuck in this immovable stranglehold whose polarizing tentacles reach into our whole society. It is imperative that we resolve this logjam issue.

20 years ago—can it be that long?—I first wrote an

article printed in the Florida State *Flambeau*, entitled: "Is there a peaceable solution for the abortion war without compromise?" It was described, as now, to be the issue that won't go away—as divisive as slavery before the Civil War.

Who is listening and who wants peace? I'm sure most people do—many feel as I do. We hear this word, "Civility"—we lament its lack in the way we deal with our differences.

> "War has always had an adversary who hardly ever comes forward as such but does its work in the stillness. This adversary is speech, the speech of genuine conversation in which people understand one another and come to mutual understanding. . .the abysses between man and man threatens ever more pitilessly to become unbridgeable." – Martin Buber

Unbridgeable.

We are the people and our collective consciousness is reflected in Washington. The best of leaders is hindered in this toxic climate of non-listening and false accusation. Our nation is . . . so fractured.

Once I stayed at the historic Beacon Hill Friend's Home in Boston. When the director showed me the library, I was eager to explore. The first book to draw my attention was *Five Present Day Controversies*, by Charles Jefferson. I opened at random:

> "The mind of the average man today is confused. That is because we are living in a hurry. We have no time to listen to anything through, or to read anything through, or to think anything through. We have a multitude of counselors, and the air is filled with voices, which are saying things. We snatch up a sentence today, and another one tomorrow, and we have no time to put the two sentences together. . The world is flooded with papers and magazines and books. . ."

I flipped over a few pages:

"And where are we to look for relief? Certainly not to the national Government. There is no balm in that Gilead. Our Government is so constructed that a little company of foolish and stubborn men can tie it into a hard knot, so that democracy is incapable of functioning at all. The national government is paralyzed again and again by the spirit of partisanship. What can we do to help us out of our distresses?

"We cannot go to the courts. Our Secretary of State, Mr. Hughes, said the other day that we make twelve thousand new laws every year in this country. He called attention to the confusion resulting from clashing interpretations and judgments. The processes of our judicature are so technical and complicated, that lawsuits drag on interminably. Many of our leading lawyers have been telling us for years that a poor man stands little chance of getting justice in our courts.

"We cannot go to our churches. The Churches are numerous and active, but they are unable to focus their moral forces on the spot where it is most needed. We have all sorts of organizations created for numberless good purposes, but all of them are impotent..."

Again I flipped over more pages:

"You cannot argue with men who are afraid. Under the spell of fear men will do all sorts of foolish things..."

The copyright of this up-to-date book is 1924. What,

4

before television and the Internet there were the same kinds of people and challenges?

> "Television atomizes, compartmentalizes, manipulates, disjoins, disintegrates, wrenches from context, ignores, and changes the subject whenever it feels like it. It does not sit still for complex arguments"—Eric Alterman

However, let's stand on the shoulders of those who have gone before us and determine to "sit still for complex arguments." Our lives, being so full of stimulus, it can be hard to do the very necessary reflection and inward listening. The healing of our nation depends on it.

Before we can have a healing journey, we must have a **hearing** journey. We come from different backgrounds with different experiences. This should be an asset to enlarge our perceptions as we listen to one another, giving and receiving—not, as it is, a liability dividing and destroying.

I pray the energy be defused around this deadly gridlock—that we may be free to do our necessary work unhindered..

> "*Be swift to hear and slow to speak*" James 1:19

> "*Don't just look on your own things but on the things of others*" Philippians 2:4

> "*He that answereth a matter before he hears it, to him it is folly and shame*" Proverbs 18:13

> "If you would convince me of error, you must first demonstrate you heard what I said"-- Charles Finney

> "*Do violence to no man, neither accuse any falsely. . .*" Luke 3:14

The above quotations can apply to any issue considered. If

our thinking could be so changed as to end this abortion impasse, the skills learned would be reflected in our other differences as well.

Single issue advocacy is always detrimental—looking only out of my own window in narrowness of focus. I live in New York, said to be the capital of the world. In a sense you can go all over the world and be in this one place. I love to talk to people of different cultures—from "faraway places with strange sounding names".

Well, what are you? Hurry, tell me. Pro-Life, Pro-Choice, Anti-abortion, Pro-abortion? I want to know which button to push so I, like a computer, can spiel off my beliefs and tell you what I think of the other side.

I am none of these, and yet, perhaps, all of them. These labels are worn and convoluted. We are weary of them. Will you, with me, throw them in the river and begin anew? A new title—a new label—for a new day seeing with new eyes. I am

La Verde de la Vida.

from The Greatest Thing in the World, Henry Drummond (1851-1897)

To love abundantly is to live abundantly, and to love for ever is to live forever. Hence, eternal life is inextricably bound up with love...

...Be not deceived. The words which all of us shall one day hear sound not of theology, but of life, not of churches and saints, but of the hungry and the poor, not of creeds and doctrines but of shelter and clothing, not of Bibles and prayer books but of cups of cold water...

In the book of Matthew, where the Judgment Day is depicted for us in the imagery of One seated upon a throne, and dividing the sheep from the goats, the test of a man is then not, "How have I believed?" but "How have I loved?" The test of religion, the final test of religion is not religiousness, but Love...

Christ did not come into the world to give man religion... The tendency of the religions of all time has been to care more for religion than for humanity...

The world in which we live is an unfinished world. It is not wise, it is not happy, it is not pure, it is not good... Humanity is little more than raw material. Almost everything has yet to be done to it... The work of Creation is going on... And this teeming universe of people in which we live has almost all its finer color and beauty yet to take... The fires of its passion were not yet cool; their heat had to be transformed into finer energies... the forces to realize them were not yet born... God's way of making worlds is to make them make themselves... God does not grudge souls their comfort... Be sure that wherever religion appears small, or forbidding, or narrow, or inhuman, you are dealing not with the whole... Not even with an arch or column—every detail is perfect—but with some cold stone removed from its place and suggesting nothing of the glorious structure from which it came.

This programme deals with a real world. Think of it as you read—not of the surface-world, but of the world as it is, as it sins and weeps, and curses and suffers and sends up it long cry to God. Limit it, if you like, to the world around your door, but think of it—of the city and the hospital and the dungeon and the graveyard, of the sweating shops and the pawn shops and the drink shops: think of the cold, the cruelty the fever, the famine, the ugliness, the loneliness, the pain. And then try to keep down the lump in your throat as you take up His Programme and read—

> *To bind up the Broken Hearted:*
> *To proclaim Liberty to the Captives:*
> *To comfort all that Mourn:*
> *To give unto them—*
> *Beauty for Ashes,*
> *The Oil of Joy for Mourning,*
> *The garment of Praise for the Spirit of Heaviness.*

What an exchange—beauty for ashes, joy for mourning, liberty for chains...

And that is the work of the Day of Vengeance. What is that day? It is now... Wherever the poor are trodden upon... wherever the air is poison and the water foul; wherever want stares, and vice reigns, and rags rot—there the Avenger takes his stand. Whatever makes it more difficult for the drunkard to reform, for the children to be pure, for the widow to earn a wage, for any of these wheels of progress to revolve...with these he deals. Delay him not. He is the messenger of God... Though evil stalks the world, it is on the way to execution; though wrong reigns, it must end in self-combustion... God might have done all this work Himself, with His own hands, but He did not. The crowning wonder of His scheme is that He entrusted it to people...

Noah Goes to the Aquarium

It is an ambitious field trip for Imagine, the day care of my two year old grandson, Noah, to go all the way to the Aquarium from Brooklyn Heights, the top of Brooklyn to Coney Island at the bottom of Brooklyn. In fact, it will require three subways. My daughter, Rebecca, has asked me to go with them and I am happy to do so.

There is much excitement this morning as adults are telling the toddlers, "We're going to go on the subway train. We're going to see fish."

Noah likes to repeat what he's told—which may be one reason he learns so fast, "See fish. Subway train, choo choo!" So with little legs walking and holding hands, we are off.

I have three children and Noah is my seventh grandchild-- I've been taking care of him around two days a week since his birth. It seems that more than ever before, I am aware of how impressionable babies and crawlers and toddlers are as they discover and see things for the first time I am fascinated to watch Noah explore and investigate and see his reactions.

With abandon, he expresses his emotions. Always, he's been a loud crier. However, likewise his laughter bubbles over with such delight, especially when he's running to meet his Mommy or Daddy coming home—surely there's nothing more wonderful to hear—and when he giggles--Noah, spontaneous, loving and sweet.

He's also quite adept at saying, "No!" How shall I describe the many ways he says it? Sometimes stubborn. Sometimes authoritatively bossing the cat, "No, cat! No, Charleston!" Every now and then I have to turn my face away to smile by the way he draws out "No-o-o-o"--maybe to another child seeking to push ahead of him going up the slide—that determination—that little look in his eye as though he were a powerful force instead of just a little mite.

On occasion, standing still, as though studying something, his little brow thinking, you can almost see the wheels going around and you wonder what he's putting together in his head.

9

Delighting us, his first word was unique. "Apple!" he said one day pointing. These days it almost takes your breath away-- he's learning new words daily and often says things I didn't know he knew the words for—you're growing up fast, Noah. I see eight year olds and think... I see teenagers on the subway and realize... and one day... With my children and grandchildren, I've seen this happen. And so quickly, it seems.

"*What manner of child shall this be*" (Luke 1:66). What is he supposed to do in the world? What are his abilities and talents? I'm secretly hoping (well, not so secretly—I've voiced it and I've been showing Noah a DVD of Andre Rieu playing his violin with his orchestra) that Noah will start violin lessons when he is three—my father was a musician.

And I will never forget when he said, out of the blue, "I love you, Mimi." It was the first full sentence I heard him say.

On this trip I am aware of how we love to see things fresh and new through a child's eyes. We can hardly wait to show them things and bring home presents, especially of things they've never seen before.

We're eager to see their response—to see what they will do—what they will say—to laugh with them.

Always Noah is very much "in the moment" going down a street, stopping to look at whatever draws his fancy, no sense of time. His eyes take in everything. He points out things which I, with familiarity, miss. What a responsibility to know his eyes are seeing; his ears are hearing; he's getting his first impressions of how the world is. There's a song:

> *Oh, be careful little ears what you hear*
> *Oh, be careful, little eyes what you see*

It's actually a song for us. Little ones can't help what they see and hear. We must be careful what they see and hear and experience. Is this what we want them to learn? Is this the impression we want them to have?

Successfully getting everyone on and off of the trains, we are now walking toward the boardwalk. Noah looks over, "Roller Coaster"(I didn't know he knew what a roller coaster was!) "School bus." and then, "Ocean."

At last,—the Aquarium! Seeing fish in an aquarium is nothing new to me, but now I can hardly wait because I am with Noah.. How eager is Noah and what wonder in his eyes! Going under and climbing up, he manages to get himself as close as possible to the fish behind the glass. What a happy crowd! Adults excitedly pointing out things, children repeating, jumping up and down. "What a big turtle—he's looking right at you! He's waving to say "Hi!" "Hi Turtle!" "Bye Shark!" We must say "Hi!" and "Bye!" to everything—it's a friendly world!

One of the first things we see is a Walrus. A parent behind us is calling out, "Marcus, it's a Walrus! Marcus, it's a Walrus!" And though he doesn't know Marcus and is just now finding out what a Walrus is himself, to my amazement Noah turns around from his on-the-ledge-vantage point to affirm and to help get the message out that yes, indeed, "Marcus, it's a Walrus!" exclaims Noah. (You would have to realize his age and hear his voice to fully appreciate how very cute this is!)

Full of adventure Noah, on the way home, falls asleep on my lap. Is there anything more heavenly than a sleeping child?

On this trip I am, of course, seeing through Noah's eyes. But I have also been seeing through the eyes of mothers and children I have only read about—Other children, newly born so fresh from heaven, what do their eyes see, what are their first experiences? Hunger, screaming, bombs falling? What do their parents have to show them? To give them? What kind of life are they born into? Little ones Noah's age?   I have been writing in my head.

When my oldest daughter, Jacinda, held newborn, Abigail, my first grandchild, she looked down at her and said, "I don't want anything bad ever to happen to you, Abby." Is this not the feeling of mothers everywhere? .

A sleeping child is heavy. Carrying him from the subway to Imagine someone, noticing Noah is heavy for me, offers to take a turn with me. When we return, he awakes as she lays him on his cot.   Startled out of sleep and seeing I am no longer holding him, he cries out. I go to him to calm him. The day care worker assures me, "He'll be all right." And I think he will—after all, though he has just moved up from the Sunfish to the Turtles

11

a few days ago, he is in familiar surroundings and he loves his Day Care. So I leave. But I listen outside the door. I go to the rest room and come back. He is still crying. I know the daycare worker is comforting him, but his heartbroken cries tear at my heart and I am feeling with him. We've shared this whole exciting day-- then to awaken suddenly out of mid-sleep somehow disorients him—to see me go. As any parent knows, there are different kinds of crying—some crying not to be humored at all, but this is different. I wish I had stayed beside him until he went back to sleep. But now to go in would make things worse. I wait outside the door until he is settled.

But again, I compare my situation, Noah's situation, with the children of war torn countries, places where children are not safe—where children go to sleep and wake up in dangerous, unfamiliar places with no mother near, to cry and have no mother come. "*What manner of child is this*?" Shouldn't this be a question asked about every child? What are they supposed to do in the world and how can we help them do it? I compare this pain in my heart and realize how small this distress—it is nothing—nothing at all. Because, of course, Noah is very safe. He will wake up in safe places with plenty to eat.

And sure enough when Rebecca and I pick up Noah a few hours later, he is full of sunshine, running and laughing and telling his mother, "Shark! Big turtle! Subway train!"

The Links

To expand our horizons –to put the parts in the whole-- I want to go around the world.   As Chief Seattle is supposed to have said, "All things are connected". We want to get totally away from single issue advocacy. Martin Buber said, "God speaks in the guise of everything that happens." So we listen, letting the pieces, as a kaleidoscope, fall where they may, making patterns as they turn, as they link and touch and relate. Like the wind, the Spirit directs, joins and separates, opens and closes...

"Right now
A child
is crying. . .
Right now
a child
is suffering
Right now
a child
is dying. . .
Every 3 seconds a child under the age of 5 dies. ..
24,000, a day dying from preventable causes. . .
Nearly 9 million a year. ..
We know what it takes
and it is not hard and it is not expensive:
safe, clean water
skilled birth attendants
good nutrition
access to health care. . ."
World Vision

*What's Going On?
Child Soldiers in Sierra Leone
30,000 child soldiers in other countries

*A Child's Choice
Countless children have three fates:
war,
drugs,
prostitution.
100 million children are unable to attend school.

There are more than 100 million street children around the world who live in fear every day of their lives. According to Amnesty international, many of these children "disappear," are beaten, illegally detained and confined, sexually exploited, tortured and systematically killed by agents of the state.

For innumerable children water is costly, dirty and scarce.

14

* Women worldwide are dying of pregnancy-related causes at a rate of about one a minute Many are too far away from a hospital.

> It's appalling how many women are dying in the United States from complications due to pregnancy and childbirth. The shocking truth behind these numbers is that half of these can be prevented.

> These women are dying because they have no access to health care or maternal care. In fact, 13 million women between the ages of 15-44—that one in 5 women of reproductive age-- have no health insurance at all.   Many begin pregnancy with untreated or unmanaged conditions that only get worse with pregnancy. . .
> Christ   McGraw   Program   Director   Grassroots Advocacy
> *Amnesty International USA*

*"Did you know that Hunger is Afghanistan's Biggest Killer?"
AOL News, by Samuel Loewenberg, Novembe 6,2009

> Death   by   violence   has   become   tragically commonplace in Afghanistan -- for Afghans, foreign troops and aid organizations alike. But a far more efficient killer stalks the Afghan people: hunger. . . An estimated 1.2 million children younger than 5 and 550,000 pregnant or lactating mothers are at risk of falling into severe malnutrition. The country has the third highest child mortality rate in the world: More than 300,000 children five and younger die each year.

Children of the Taliban (video, PBS):
http://www.pbs.org/frontlineworld/stories/pakistan802/

> 25 children appear wearing the traditional Pakistani shalwar kameez. Sitting cross-legged on the ground, they rock back and forth reciting the Koran... Housed in a bare compound, three young boys watch over the group holding automatic guns.

Their teacher, dressed in brown military fatigues, paces the room reading from a book called, "Justifications for Suicide Bombing." Moving to a white board, he writes, "Reasons for killing a spy." ...Three teenage boys talk about their desire to become suicide bombers. We meet Zainullah, who later blows himself up killing six; then Sadique, who blows himself up killing 22; and Masood who kills 28. We're shown footage glorifying their attacks... "Suicide" schools run by the Taliban are preparing a generation of boys to commit atrocities against civilians. Last year, suicide attacks struck right across Pakistan, killing more than 800 people. Pakistan's war is no longer confined to the lawless Tribal areas along the Afghan border, it has moved to the cities. Children are being killed, but they are also being turned into killers... [from transcript]

*"Divorced Before Puberty," by Nicholas Kristof, *New York Times*, March 8, 2010

It's hard to imagine that there have been many younger divorcées — or braver ones — than a pint-size third grader named Nujood. Nujood is a Yemeni girl, and it's no coincidence that Yemen abounds both in child brides and in terrorists (and now, thanks to Nujood, children who have been divorced).Societies that repress women tend to be prone to violence.

For Nujood, the nightmare began at age 10 when her family told her that she would be marrying a deliveryman in his 30s. Although Nujood's mother was unhappy, she did not protest. "In our country it's the men who give the orders, and the women who follow them,"

Nujood writes in a powerful new autobiography just published in the United States this week, "I Am Nujood, Age 10 and Divorced." Her new husband forced her to drop out of school (she was in the second grade) because a married woman shouldn't be a student. At her wedding, Nujood sat in the corner, her face swollen from crying.

Nujood's father asked the husband not to touch her until a year after she had had her first menstrual period. But as soon as they were married, she writes, her husband forced himself on her. He soon began to beat her as well, the memoir says, and her new mother-in-law offered no sympathy. "Hit her even harder," the mother-in-law would tell her son.

Nujood had heard that judges could grant divorces, so one day she sneaked away, jumped into a taxi and asked to go to the courthouse.

"I want to talk to the judge," the book quotes Nujood as forlornly telling a woman in the courthouse.

"Which judge are you looking for?"

"I just want to speak to a judge, that's all."

"But there are lots of judges in this courthouse."

"Take me to a judge — it doesn't matter which one!"

When she finally encountered a judge, Nujood declared firmly: "I want a divorce!"

So educating Nujood and giving her a chance to become a lawyer — her dream — isn't just a matter of fairness. It's also a way to help tame the entire country... little girls like Nujood may prove more effective than missiles at defeating terrorists.

*"Another Tragic Child Bride Story in Yemen," by Dana Kennedy,

Contributor *AOL News*

> (April 9, 2010 New York Times) – A 12-year-old
> Yemeni girl has died of internal bleeding caused by
> intercourse during her wedding night after being
> married off to a much older man, the latest in a series
> of tragic stories involving the country's child brides.

* "Amid Abuse in Brazil, Abortion Debate Flares," by Alexei Barriionuevo
New York Times, March 27, 2009

> . . . Weighing just 79 pounds and barely four feet tall,
> the 9-year-old girl, from Alagoinha, a town in the
> northeast, underwent an abortion when she was 15
> weeks pregnant. . . A Brazilian archbishop summarily
> excommunicated everyone involved — the doctors
> for performing the abortion and the girl's mother for
> allowing it — except for the stepfather, who stands
> accused of raping the girl over a number of years...

*"Nun Excommunicated For Abortion Decision To Save Mother's Life,"
by David Gibson, www.politicsdaily.com

> When it comes to Catholic teaching on abortion,
> no exceptions are allowed. Even if carrying a
> pregnancy to term would result in the death of both
> mother and child, abortion is still not an option.
> Which is why a nun who is an administrator at
> a Catholic hospital in Phoenix this week found
> herself formally excommunicated -- essentially the
> sacramental equivalent of capital punishment...

"Sister Margaret's Choice," by Nicholas Kristof, *New York Times*, May
26, 2010

> We finally have a case where the Roman Catholic
> Church hierarchy is responding forcefully and speedily
> to allegations of wrongdoing.

> But the target isn't a pedophile priest. Rather, it's a
> nun who helped save a woman's life. Doctors describe
> her as saintly.

The excommunication of Sister Margaret McBride in Phoenix underscores all that to me feels morally obtuse about the church hierarchy. I hope that a public outcry can rectify this travesty. . .

*"A Heartbreaking Choice:" Mothers tell their stories of heartbreak. Read their stories before jumping to judgment. *www.aheartbreakingchoice.com/kansasstories*

The reality was that at the most painful time of my life I had to travel out of state, stay in a hotel room and face hostile protesters...

*An Open Letter to Politicians

I am writing this letter to you to share the story of my daughter Emilee Nicole. I am a life long Maryland resident and until recently was very proud to live here. My husband and I have a two year old little girl and decided that it was time to try again. We were very exited to learn that we would be having another little girl at our 21-week ultrasound.

What should have been a routine visit turned out to be our worst nightmare. . .

*from *The Audacity of Hope* by Barak Obama:

. . .Most antiabortion activists, for example, have openly discouraged legislative allies from even pursuing those compromise measures that would have significantly reduced the incidence of the procedure popularly known as partial-birth abortion, because the image the procedure evokes in the mind of the public has helped them win converts to their position. And sometimes our ideological predispositions are just so fixed that we have trouble seeing the obvious. . .ideology overrides whatever facts call theory into question. . .as a member of the Illinois legislature I had argued for an amendment to include a mother's health exception in a Republican bill to ban partial-birth abortion. The amendment failed on a party line vote, and afterward, I stepped out into the hallway with one of my Republican colleagues. Without the amendment, I said, the law would be struck down by the courts as unconstitutional. He turned to me and said it didn't matter what amendment was attached— judges would do whatever they wanted to do anyway. "It's all politics," he had said, turning to leave. "And right now we've got the votes."

As you can see, what really happened gets twisted to give the wrong impression for political advantage.

*Letter to Help Baby Margaret Grace& St. Vincent's Hospital
From assistant pastor of First Presbyterian Church, Brooklyn

January 27, 2010
Dear Friends
We urgently need your help to fight against the immanent closure of St. Vincent's Hospital in Greenwich Village. St. Vincent's has been struggling with financial problems. ...

This issue is personal for us. Our daughter, Margaret Grace, is a patient in the Neonatal Intensive Care Unit--one of the units that would be closed. We will be seriously affected by this.

Why is St. Vincent's worth fighting for? When we experienced a sudden rupture of Beth's amniotic sac at 18 weeks, our doctor (affiliated with another NYC hospital) dropped us from care when we said we would not terminate the pregnancy. Doctors at St. Vincent's took us in and gave us the care and encouragement we needed. The doctors and nurses in the NICU have treated us--and Grace--like family. The NICU at St. Vincent's takes in dozens of children and parents whom other hospitals have given up on. Three of our NICU mates fall into this category and are thriving.

One mother has been pregnant for the last 4 years always delivering days shy of 24 weeks. At the 2 other NYC hospitals she tried, they let her first 3 babies go because of hospital policy not to intervene. Tomorrow she takes home a healthy baby whom St. Vincent's was willing to treat despite being born at 23+weeks. For babies that won't make it, St Vincent's offers a Neonatal Hospice program with free counseling, free care by the chief neonatologist, extra support for single mothers, mahogany infant caskets, and free cemetery plots from the Sisters of Charity. As people of faith who believe in the right to choose, we were shocked to find ourselves and other parents who found they weren't given a choice at other hospitals. We wanted the opportunity to parent our child with integrity through our pregnancy and possibly short life. St. Vincent's was the only place we found would do that..

Beyond our personal investment, St. Vincent's mission matters to this city. Founded on 13th Street in 1849, St. Vincent's was founded to provide care for our community's poorest residents. It's mission continues to affirm that ministry: Saint Vincent Catholic Medical Centers is committed to reflecting God's love by advancing Christ's healing ministry, with Respect, Integrity, Compassion and Excellence to all who come to us in need, especially the poor. In 2008 alone, St. Vincent's provided $46 million in medical care to the homeless and poor of our city. It serves 65,000 in its ER. It has one of the largest HIV/AIDS clinics.

Help St. Vincent's keep fighting to stay open by...

"St. Vincent's Closes for Good," NBC New York Apr 30, 2010
> An emergency room sign was removed and "closed" signs were posted on its double doors.

As you can see, St. Vincent's closed. Margaret Grace was in the hospital

6 months, was transferred to another hospital. When she goes home, she will need 24/7 care.

*"Learning from the Sin of Sodom," by Nicholas Kristof, *New York Times*

> A growing number of conservative Christians are acknowledging that to be "pro-life" must mean more than opposing abortion . . . Evangelicals have become the new internationalists, pushing successfully for new American programs against AIDS and malaria, and doing superb work on issues from human trafficking in India to mass rape in Congo.
>
> A pop quiz: What's the largest U.S.-based international relief and development organization? It's not Save the Children, and it's not CARE — both terrific secular organizations. Rather, it's World Vision, a Seattle-based Christian organization (with strong evangelical roots) whose budget has roughly tripled over the last decade...
>
> The head of World Vision in the United States, Richard Stearns, begins his fascinating book, The Hole in Our Gospel, with an account of a visit a decade ago to Uganda, where he met a 13-year-old AIDS orphan who was raising his younger brothers by himself.
>
> "What sickened me most was this question: where was the Church?" he writes. "Where were the followers of Jesus Christ in the midst of perhaps the greatest humanitarian crisis of our time? Surely the Church should have been caring for these *'orphans and widows in their distress.'* (James 1:27). Shouldn't the pulpits across America have flamed with exhortations to rush to the front lines of compassion?
>
> "How have we missed it so tragically, when even rock stars and Hollywood actors seem to understand?"

Mr. Stearns argues that evangelicals were often so focused on sexual morality and a personal relationship with God that they ignored the needy. He writes laceratingly about "a Church that had the wealth to build great sanctuaries but lacked the will to build schools, hospitals, and clinics."

In one striking passage, Mr. Stearns quotes the prophet Ezekiel as saying that the great sin of the people of Sodom wasn't so much that they were promiscuous or gay as that they were "arrogant, overfed and unconcerned; they did not help the poor and needy."

"Behold, this was the iniquity of thy sister Sodom, pride, fullness of bread, and abundance of idleness was in her and in her daughters, neither did she strengthen the hand of the poor and needy." (Ezekiel 16:49).

*"For Ex-G.O.P. Official, Obama Is Candidate of Catholic Values," *New York Times*, August 29, 2008

When Douglas W. Kmiec endorsed Senator Barak Obama for president last spring, it made waves, especially among Roman Catholics.

A constitutional scholar who headed the Office of Legal Counsel under Presidents Ronald Reagan and George Bush, Mr. Kmiec was well known as an articulate opponent of abortion...

> Q. Given those views, why do you support Barack Obama?
>
> A. There is a widespread misconception that overturning Roe is the only way to be pro-life... I doubt that many of our non-legally-trained pro-life friends fully grasps the limited effect of overturning Roe... Senator Obama is articulating policies that permit faithful Catholics to follow the church's admonition that we continue to explore ways to give greater protection to human life.
>
> Consider the choices: A Catholic can either continue on the failed and uncertain path of seeking to overturn Roe, which would result in the individual states doing their own thing... Or Senator Obama's approach could be followed, whereby prenatal and income support, paid maternity leave and greater access to adoption

would be relied upon to reduce the incidence of abortion... There are clearly partisan forces that want nothing more than to manufacture or stir up faith-based opposition to their political opponents.

*The President Speaks at Notre Dame, 350,000 sign online petition opposing

Listen to opposing views:

Listen first to Fr. Corapi of The Cardinal Newman Society—You Tube: Obama Notre Dame Scandal or NotreDameScandel.com www. CardinalNewmanSociety.org

Then listen to President Obama: In Praise of Fair Minded Words at Notre Dame posted by Jess Lee—The Whitehouse: Obama answers Notre Dame Hecklers with 'fair-minded words. . . www.whitehouse. gov/.../Remarks-by-the-President-at-Notre-Dame-Commencement/ - May 17, 2009. . .The speech underlined the president's desire to elevate public discourse on issues such as abortion in order to find common ground. www.csmonitor.com/.../obama-answers-notre-dame-hecklers-with-fair-minded-word.

(You will be impressed with Notre Dame's enthusiasm for the President... His speech is masterful. As you listen prayerfully with your heart, you will know God's answer.)

*"President Obama's Faith Based Initiatives," *New York Times*, February 5, 2009

President Obama appointed Joshua DuBois, a former associate pastor and advisor to the President in the U.S. Senate office and campaign Director of Religious Affairs, to lead this office. "Joshua understands the issues at stake, knows the people involved. . .It will be one voice among several in the administration that will look at how we support women and children and address teenage pregnancy and reduce the need for abortion...

There will be 25 members of the council.

...After the election, the Rev. Jay Scott Newman told his South Carolina parishioners they should not take communion if they voted for "Barack Hussein Obama" because "our nation has chosen for its chief executive the most radical pro-abortion politician ever to serve in the United states Senate or to run for president" www.nytimes.com/2009/12/06/us/06threat.html

It might be tempting to dismiss these statements as the work of a few well-placed cranks, congressmen and clergy. But the Secret Service reported more threats against Obama than any other president-elect. Christopher Hewitt, Political Violence and Terrorism in Modern America: A Chronology (Santa Barbara, CO: Praeger Security International, 2005), pp.28-90

The politics of hate has a trickle-down effect, as the residents of Madison County, Idaho, found out days after the election when a school bus full of second- and third-graders chanted "assassinate Obama." Richard Hofstadter, The Paranoid Style in American Politics (New York: Vintage Books, 2008), pp.23, 24

Praying for the President's Death

"I hate Barack Obama. You say, well, you just mean you don't like what he stands for. NO, I hate the person. Oh, you mean you just don't like his policies. NO, I hate him. . I am not going to pray for his good. I am going to pray that he dies and goes to hell." http://washingtonindependent. com/61229/more-trent-franks-the-president-is-an-enemy-of-humanity

Here endeth the lesson at the Faithful Word Baptist Church in Tempe, Arizona. L That's where Pastor Steven L. Anderson fired off a straight-to-the –point sermon on Sunday, August 16, 2009, titled "Why I Hate Barack Obama."

"Obama is overturning the U.S. Constitution,

overturning everything we believe as a country, overturning some 200 years of history," Anderson thundered from the pulpit. "He is the revolutionary and it's a socialist/communist revolution. We are the counter-revolutionaries saying no, we don't want a change." He even offered parishioners a view into his own private Obama prayer: "Break his teeth, oh God, in his mouth; as a snail which melteth , let him pass away; like an untimely birth of a woman −that he thinks—he calls it a woman's right to choose, you know, he thinks it's so wonderful he ought to be aborted. It ought to be, 'Abort Obama, that ought to be the motto."

Note: People who think President Obama wishes to overturn the Constitution need to read his book, *Audacity of Hope*. He taught the Constitution. You will be impressed that probably very few presidents have had his knowledge and love of our founding documents.

* *Need to Know,* PBS, "Essay: A New Season of Hate in America," May 13, 2010

Anger is perhaps America's oldest collective national emotion. Without it there might not be a United States at all. But there have been times when the force that perennially divides us is not anger, as much as its more violent and more disturbing cousin — hate.

In this essay, Need to Know co-host Jon Meacham takes a look back at moments in American history when hate has exploded in violence and across the national consciousness, and to recent expressions of it against members of Congress.

*"Texas Lawmaker Admits 'Baby Killer' Remark," by Carl Hulse, *New York Times*, May 19, 2010

Representative Randy Neugebauer, a conservative Republican from Texas, revealed on Monday that he was the lawmaker who shouted "baby killer" on the House floor Sunday night as Representative Bart Stupak, a Michigan Democrat, discussed abortion-related aspects of the health care legislation. . .

*"Distant Wars, Constant Ghosts," by Shannon P. Meehan, New York Times, February 22, 2010
Features the writing of men and women who have returned from wartime service in the United States military.

Since the two recent NATO-led military strikes that accidentally killed dozens of Afghan civilians, I have been thinking a great deal about the psychic toll that killing takes on soldiers.

In 2007, I was an Army lieutenant leading a group on a house-clearing mission in Baquba, Iraq, when I called in an artillery strike on a house. I thought we had struck enemy fighters, but I was wrong. A father, mother and their children had been huddled inside. The feelings of disbelief that initially filled me quickly transformed into feelings of rage and self-loathing.

*"Haiti's Children Adrift in World of Chaos," New York Times, July 11, 2010

Not long after 14-year-old Daphne Joseph escaped her collapsed house on the day of the earthquake, she boarded a crowded jitney with her uncle and crawled in traffic toward the capital, where her single mother sold beauty products in the Tête Boeuf marketplace. "Mama," she said she repeated to herself. "Mama, I'm coming."

Abandoning the slow-moving jitney, Daphne, petite and delicate, got separated from her uncle and jumped onto a motorcycle-for-hire. She arrived alone at a marketplace in ruins and ran, in her dusty purple sandals, toward a pile of debris laced with "broken people," she said.

Growing closer, she saw her mother, lifeless. She froze, she said, eventually watching as her mother's body was dumped in a wheelbarrow and her only parent vanished into the chaos. . .

*The Hook- ESSAY- *Bloody Kansas*: Why incivility can be dangerous. www.readthehook.com. Charlottesville, VA based weekly publication offering News and Culture coverage.

Before The Civil War...

Having now attempted to hear John Yoo speak and having learned that someone cut a gas line he or she thought fed the home of Congressman Tom Perriello, I wonder if we are on the verge of another clash brought on by the people who deny those of us in the middle our right to think and act upon our own. Tea Partiers, I read in my morning newspaper, are seeking to drown out the president's speech in Iowa, and someone threw a brick through the Albemarle County Republicans' office window.

What is it, I wonder, about we as a people that we seems incapable of keeping the fringe thinkers on the fringes? Why do we so quickly allow them to dominate our political conversations and turn reasonable discussion into shouting, angry battles?

Why do we seem incapable of understanding that all of the issues facing our nation are complex and that only rational dialogue has any chance of solving them without bloodshed?...

Why do we in the media seemingly give the microphone to the craziest voices we can find?

The media's common refrain is that conflict is "news."

It's what the people want; what they demand or they'll change channels. . .Information must be, we media people in the age of television and internet think, fascinating or entertaining-- or the audience's little brains will tune it out.

We in the media have gradually concluded that complexity is beyond our audience's capabilities...

The best shout in bumper sticker length gets the ink— or the infamous 15 minutes of "fame" – therefore pushing the shouting radicals even further towards acting on their poorly analyzed political dogma...

A former journalism teacher at Virginia Union University, Randy Salzman.

A Walk to Beautiful. www.youtube.com; http://www.pbs.org/wgbh/nova.
A difficult journey that begins in loneliness and shame for thousands of Ethiopian women ends in a productive new life and hope for the future in this award-winning film.

Beginning transcript:
NARRATOR: Funding for A Walk to Beautiful is provided by The Fistula Foundation . . . A complete list is available from PBS.
AYEHU'S MOTHER: I, her mother, made her live out back.
AYEHU (Fistula Patient): I was very upset at having to deal with people's disgust and disdain for me, so I decided to go and make a shelter and wait for certain death.
AYEHU'S MOTHER: If she were not sick, I would not have her separate from me.
AYEHU: The labor lasted for a week. The baby died in my womb. After the doctor took it out, I felt something leaking.

I was living with my husband when I got this problem. He told me to leave, and he married someone else. So I took my daughter and came to live here in this condition.

AYEHU'S MOTHER: It's very difficult to let her stay in the house, because people come to visit.

AYEHU: I have no married life. I don't have a job, I don't mix with people. I live here hidden away from others. This is not life. Death would be better than this.FIKRE: (Former Fistula Patient): The baby had died in my womb. The doctor took out the body piece by piece.

I started sleeping on the ground, because I was wetting my bed. For 10 years I lived like this.

Good morning. How are you?

AYEHU: I am fine.

FIKRE: Are you feeling better?

AYEHU: I'm okay.

FIKRE: I remember when everybody used to shun me, especially on the bus, where people covered their noses because of the stench. I would get so hurt and ashamed. After the surgery, I have become a normal person, wearing new clothes and mixing with friends.

Illegal Abortions a Major Killer of Women in Ethiopia

According to the World Health organization, complications arising from illegal abortions are now the second leading cause of death for young women in Ethiopia. Only tuberculosis kills more young women in that poverty-stricken nation. . .

*"Jamaican Doctor Accused of Abortion on 13-Year-Old," WORLD, February 19, 2010

KINGSTON, Jamaica (AP) -- Authorities in Jamaica are investigating a doctor who has been accused of performing an illegal abortion on a 13-year-old girl.

*HEALTH / HEALTH CARE POLICY. November 08, 2009. "Abortion Was at Heart of Wrangling," by David M. Herszenhorn and Jackie Calmes

*"Palin Criticizes Obama on Abortion," by Brenda Farrington, August 26, 2010

> JACKSONVILLE, Fla. — Sarah Palin called President Barack Obama the most pro-abortion president ever Thursday and mocked Florida's governor for claiming to be pro-life after vetoing a bill that would have required women to get ultrasounds before having the procedure.
>
> In a speech that only ventured into politics on abortion issues, Palin criticized Obama's health care overhaul as a plan that will lead to more abortions.
>
> "The biggest advance of the abortion industry in America is the passage of Obamacare," Palin said. "Elective abortions have nothing to do with health care. It's about ending lives, not saving lives. . .

Palin spoke to a crowd of about 500 at a fundraiser for Heroic Media, a group that uses billboards, television ads and the internet to try direct women to crisis pregnancy centers instead of opting for abortions. The event raised about $50,000.

*"Abortion is never the right choice. It is always a grave evil." *Lifeissues* Judi Brown, "Abortion is always wrong."

Children of the Decree by Ronnie Scheib

Florin Lepan's startling documentary *Children of the Decree* explores the plight of women under Romanian strongman Nicolae Ceaucescu's infamous Decree 770, which banned birth control and abortion. In his single-minded push to repopulate the nation with millions of little "new men" destined for greatness, Ceausescu adopted ever more grotesque, Orwellian measures. . . Only women over 40 and those who already spawned four offspring were exempt from having children. In the years following the decree's passage in 1966, the birth rate doubled. Although a huge propaganda machine touted the beauty of motherhood, existing cultural biases encouraged men to disavow all post-coital responsibility, leaving the women to "take care of it" as best they could. . . In the '80s, as the worsening economy made feeding extra mouths impossible, the undeclared war between women and the state escalated. Women suspected of interrupting their pregnancies were tortured or left untreated until they revealed who helped them. .

*What is intersex? Intersex Society of North America, from Wikipedia (I include this information as an example of our not knowing everything and the humility we should have because we don't.)

> Does ISNA advocate doing nothing when a child is born with intersex?... But in human cultures, sex categories get simplified into male, female,... unusual a combination of parts has to be, before it counts as intersex. ...And some think you have to have both ovarian and testicular tissue to count as intersex. www.isna.org/faq/what_is_intersex

> Here's what we do know: If you ask experts at medical centers how often a child is born so noticeably atypical in terms of genitalia that a specialist in sex differentiation is called in, the number comes out to about 1 in 1500 to 1 in 2000 births. But a lot more people than that are born with subtler forms of sex anatomy variations, some of which won't show up until later in life. (Alice Dreger explores this question in greater depth in her book *Hermaphrodites and Medical Invention of Sex*.)

Let's admit there are many things we don't know. For example, why does God permit Intersex babies? If we had such a baby, would we decide with surgery for a boy or girl or let the baby alone? We don't know? Well, maybe there are other things we don't know and it's all right to say, "I don't know."

At a mental health drop-in-center I met a young man named David who had been such baby. His parents and doctor had decided he would be a boy. He was one of the most unhappy persons I have ever

32

met. He told me, "I wish they had let me alone. Or at least let me be a girl—not a boy." How can we make a judgment in this case? It's all right to say, "I don't know."

*"A Crazy Dream," by Bob Herbert, *New York Times*, January 31, 2009
    A documentary about the women's peace movement in Liberia spotlights the achievement of ordinary people who courageously intervene in their own fate. This documentary shows how prayer can lead to courage and right action and bring peace.

*Bill Moyers Journal, PBS, April 2, 2010
    The United States, they report, has the greatest inequality of income of any major developed country. That's the betrayal of the American way. Where there is the most inequality of income—in the country or in the states of America, there is the most crime.

*"US notches world's highest incarceration rate," by Gail Russell Chaddock, Staff writer of *The Christian Science Monitor*. August 18, 2003.
    More than 5.6 million Americans are in prison or have served time there, according to a new report by the Justice Department released Sunday. That's 1 in 37 adults living in the United States, the highest incarceration level in the world...These new numbers are shocking enough, but what we don't see are the ripple effects of what they mean.

*"The Drug Wars," PBS, *From Religion and Ethics*, March 26, 2010
    LUCKY SEVERSON, correspondent: This war zone is not in some far off country. It's just across the border from El Paso, Texas, in Juarez, Mexico, one of the most dangerous cities in the world. . . Since Mexico's president, Felipe Calderon, declared war on the drug cartels four years ago, almost 5,000 citizens have been murdered in Juarez alone. Father Kevin Mullins knows. He's officiated at too many funerals.
    FATHER MULLINS: We've experienced 38, 40 executions just in this one parish here...
    SEVERSON: The violence has spread throughout

Mexico, but Juarez has been particularly hard hit because it's a major conduit for illegal drugs passing from Mexico into the United States. It's become a bloody battleground as cartels fighting for the huge amounts of money involved murder each other and innocent civilians.

RUBEN GARCIA (Director, Annunciation House): It is a city that has real fear, a lot of it unpredictable, a lot of it you can't put your finger on it, but its certainly something with which people live on a daily basis.

SEVERSON: Some who cross over to escape the violence come here. But most, like these folks who belong to Father Mullin's parish, are stuck in Juarez, worried first about their kids and grandkids, worried about stray bullets. . . teachers have been threatened that their students will be hurt if the teachers don't pay extortion money. . . Four of Ezekiel's extended family have been victims.

FATHER MULLINS (translating for Ezekiel): So the mother and the son were killed just before Christmas outside the old US consulate, and the week before a nephew had also been executed outside the church in San Marcos.

SEVERSON: When Juan Pablo refused to use his market as a drop-off location for suspicious packages, he was told his two kids would be killed. So the family quietly...

America's Forgotten War: A series Overview, NPR

The war on drugs has been waged for 38 years, through seven White House administrations, in foreign coca fields and on America's streets, at an estimated annual cost of $40 billion. But what has it accomplished, and where does the U.S. go from here?

Alisa Barba, Western bureau chief for NPR's National Desk, edited this series. It was produced for broadcast by Marisa Penaloza.

* "'Make Drugs Legal,' says former Mexican president," ABC News,

Conservative Mexican ex-president Vicente Fox has spoken out in favor of legalizing illegal drugs, as his country sinks ever deeper into bloody drug wars.

"What has to be made legal are the production, sale and distribution [of illegal drugs]," said Mr Fox, a former Coca Cola executive, in his weekly blog.

He says the changes have to come after years at the helm of a Mexican government cooperating with the United States's "war on drugs".

Since 2006, more than 28,000 people have been killed in deepening violence as drug gangs and mafias battle for control of shipment routes, mainly to the lucrative US market.

"We've got to see it as a strategy to fight back and break the economic structure that enables cartels to earn such tremendous profits," argued Mr Fox, a member of the National Action Party, of which current president Felipe Calderon is also a member.

Mr Fox said high taxes should be charged that would then be used to treat drug addictions.

Denouement

And so... finally, at long last, you succeed—Roe is reversed—abortion is now illegal again. Decades with trillions of dollars and hours focusing on this effort and now victory! Problem solved; Mission accomplished. You have rescued the unborn. You have stopped abortion.

Have You?

Now what?

Have you really stopped abortion?

The experience of other countries (and our own) will testify that you have not. So now how shall these anti-abortions laws be enforced? What shall be the penalties? Life imprisonment? We already incarcerate more people than any other nation.

Columbia, Mexico, Haiti, The Dominican Republic, and others—all are used to feed the United States' appetite for drugs—35 billion dollars a year and this drug war has been going on for nearly 40 years. Of course, the problem is not a lack of laws against drugs. Passing laws and dealing with symptoms will simply never bring lasting results.

Observing the suffering brought on by alcoholism, there were those who worked hard and long for Prohibition, the 18th Amendment. The worthy goal was to protect families, women and children from the evils of alcohol and to bring down crime. But instead it just brought in new gangs and gangsters who bridged the gap between supply and demand. You may have heard of the St. Valentine's Day Massacre. So after 13 long years, (1919-1932) it was repealed by the 21st amendment. However Bill Wilson's Alcoholics Anonymous, which began in 1935, continues to this day. Why the difference? Because it addressed root causes and brought results.

It remains:

The laws that will change the world
are not written on paper,
but on the heart.

*"Ye are our epistle… written not with ink, but with the
Spirit of the living God; not in tables of stone, but in fleshy tables
of the heart."* (II Corinthians 3, Jeremiah 31)

Yesterday in the park someone spoke of the book, *Working*, by Studs Terkel. Working people talk about what they do all day and how they feel about what they do. Some feel regret that they spent so much of their lives doing work they either didn't enjoy, or now feel was not worthwhile. They wish they had utilized their gifts and talents—they wish they had done what they love to do—what they were born to do.

Sometimes people give all they have for, perhaps, some goal of fame and fortune only to realize, when this is achieved, that it does not satisfy the longing in their heart or make them as happy as they thought they would be. So likewise, if efforts to reverse Roe should succeed, and the people who have mistakenly given their all to this effort—polarizing and immobilizing the country, using up resources of time and money that should have gone elsewhere—and after all this sacrifice have really not saved the unborn—in fact, they look down and see in their hand *"wood, hay, and stubble"*--this is sad to give your all to destroy the very cause you wish to help. Like a war that makes things worse—a war against terrorists that makes more terrorists. You have not only not saved the unborn, but you have made the world more of a wilderness and a more violent place for children and people everywhere. As attention was distracted, unwise decisions were made, wars were fought that shouldn't have been fought .This false focus has rippled all over the earth in its devastation. It was not just 9/11 victims who paid the price for our lack of attention, but the slain of these wars and those coming home maimed and broken—some in spirit, as well as body. Young people, who are some mother's sons and daughters. We want our sorrows to be redeemable; our tears to reap joy. There's a book title, *Don't Waste Your Sorrows*. To think, "This was a hard experience;

however, what can I learn from it? What blessings can come from this failure, this grief? How can this be redeemed? God knows. *"He is plenteous in redemption"* (Psalm 130). We must let ourselves be redeemed.

I am a mother. As President Obama, on Father's Day, quoted one author, "to have a child is to decide forever to have your heart walking around outside your body."

While I was in Miami, there were some articles entitled, "Stolen Childhood," that I could not get out of my mind. They were run on the front page every day for a week in the *Miami Herald*, June 22-27, 1987:

Children work among the flames
The rich get richer at the expense of children
A global shame, children work for pennies in dangerous jobs
Kiddie porn—it's big business in Florida
30,000 Thai children work as prostitutes
Children slaves to adult greed.

The articles were illustrated with pictures. One picture: *Young prostitutes wait under floodlights to be picked by customer at brothel.*

I stared at the picture. I wrote: Jesus said our Father is so tender He sees a sparrow fall. What must He feel for the children? Imagine your teenage daughter behind such a window with a number for "customers" to choose. Virgins bring more. Would you not be as a wild woman to get your daughter out of there? We must get resource to need. We cannot just pray, pray, pray for our own children. We must be concerned about our brother's and sister's children and the children of the world.

In the park is a monument which reads:

In Honor of
Algernon-Sydney-Sullivan
Jurist-Statesman-Orator
Born 1826—Died 1887

He reached out both hands in constant helpfulness
to his fellowman.

Erected by Citizens of New York, 1906
Frank E. Wallis, Architect

An immaculate life, devoted with never failing
fidelity to public and private trusts.

On one side of the monument is a drinking fountain for people and on the other side is one for horses—my grandson would like to play and put in his hands in the horse fountain. I've walked past this monument so many times, pausing to read it. Frequently, I write the words down in one journal after another. I think, "How wonderful to live such a life—such a worthy goal— every morning to think, "This is what I will do. With God's help, I will reach out my hands in helpfulness."

Let's review:

*Outlawing abortion with the reversal of Roe will not solve the problem or stop abortion. Instead such action would multiply the problem, distracting and tying up energy needed for the goal of reducing abortions. Romania had the most stringent anti-abortion laws--abortion was punishable by prison and torture. Yet when freedom came, records showed that Romania had a high abortion rate. Latin American countries also have strong anti-abortion laws and yet multiple dangerous illegal abortions are still performed.

*Overturning Roe would have limited effect. Douglas W. Kmiec, a constitutional scholar who headed the Office of Legal counsel under Presidents Ronald Reagan and George bush, said:

> "There is a widespread misconception that overturning Roe is the only way to be pro-life… I doubt that many of our non-legally-trained pro-life friends fully grasp the limited effect of overturning Roe… Senator Obama is articulating policies that permit faithful Catholics to follow the church's admonition that we continue to explore ways to give greater protection to human life. Consider the choices… continue on the failed and uncertain path of seeking to overturn Roe,… Or Senator Obama's approach could be followed, whereby prenatal and income support, paid maternity leave and greater access to adoption would be relied upon to reduce the incidence of abortion… There are clearly partisan forces that want nothing more than to manufacture or stir up faith-based opposition to their political opponents."

*Laura Bush in her book, *Spoken from the Heart*, says that she believes abortion should remain legal for medical reasons and other reasons. She and other people like her, who have thought this through, certainly should not be considered "pro-abortion" or so labeled.

In our political debates it is imperative for our democracy that we respect truth in presenting our opponent's view. In my lifetime I have never known anyone to be criticized so much who so little deserves it as President Obama. The oil spill spewing endlessly seems an appropriate metaphor. (http://shiningriver-sheilah.blogspot.com/2010/06/president-obama-and-poetic-significance.html) What if we got the President some say we have? There were the birthers saying the President was born in Ghana and therefore, disqualified to be President. Glenn Beck, Rush Limbaugh and other TV and radio hosts leading a mentality comparing the President to Hitler, Stalin and calling him a Communist or a Nazi. President Obama couldn't even give an inspiring speech to the school children about staying in school and working hard without some thinking he was contaminating the students. Newt Gingrich and his speech writer Vince Halley falsely accused the President of taking Jesus out of his Easter message. (http://www.2010/04/obama-edits-jesus-out-of-easter. html) It seems as though the assessments of the abortion issue have permeated our whole society.

*The President was invited to give the commencement address at Notre Dame. This caused a tremendous uproar demonizing the President, calling it a scandal--which is an example of how out of balance our society has become. There were letters and protests from 350,000 people--all because of the abortion issue. President Obama is not pro-abortion anymore than Laura Bush or me. It is past time to do some meditating as to how the fringe has plowed through our whole culture.

I pray that blind eyes be open and deaf ears unstopped to truth.

I encourage you to listen to President Obama's Notre Dame speech—in which he takes on the issue of abortion—not really the subject he would have addressed at commencement had not there been so much pandemonium. Don't take other people's word for what the President believes—Listen to him yourself. www.whitehouse.gov/.../Remarks-by-the-President-at-Notre-Dame-Commencement

"He that answereth a matter before he heareth it, it is folly and shame." Proverbs 18:13

You will be impressed with Notre Dame's enthusiasm for the President... His speech is masterful. As you listen prayerfully with your heart, you will know God's answer.

From *The Audacity of Hope* by Barak Obama
"...weary of the dead zone that politics has become, in which narrow interest vie for advantage and ideological minorities seek to impose their own versions of absolute truth...8,9

"No, what's troubling is the gap between the magnitude of our challenges and the smallness of our politics—the ease with which we are distracted by the petty and trivial, our chronic avoidance of tough decisions, our seeming inability to build a working consensus to tackle any big problem..." p. 22

*Richard Stearns, the director of World Vision, wrote in his book *The Hole in our Gospel*, after a visit to Uganda: "What sickened me most was this question: where was the Church? Where were the followers of Jesus Christ in the midst of perhaps the greatest humanitarian crisis of our time? Surely the Church should have been caring for these *'orphans and widows in their distress.'* (James 1:27). Shouldn't the pulpits across America have flamed with exhortations to rush to the frontlines of compassion? How have we missed it so tragically, when even rock stars and Hollywood actors seem to understand?" (See "Learning from the Sin of Sodom," by Nicholas Kristof, *New York Times*, February 27, 2010.)

What was the reason? Too many Evangelicals have been so focused on the useless effort of reversing Roe. Since it's been a distraction from caring about and addressing the needs of dying children, this so called "Pro-Life" campaign actually has really been "Pro-Death." "There certainly needs to be a public outcry." How can we pretend to be so concerned about silent screams when we are deaf to audible screams? People against abortion should redirect their energies.

*T.W. Wilson in his book, *The Key to Lasting Joy* , writes:
I also believe that if we're going to stand against abortion, we have a further responsibility to provide alternatives to women who are pregnant and don't want the children they're carrying. This means counseling and encouragement, medical help, financial aid, and assistance in placing children for adoption once they are born. All these services must be offered in love and

without condemnation

Roe prevents none of the above.   Efforts should be given to positive steps to reduce abortion.

* Amnesty International reports:
It's appalling how many women are dying in the United States from complications due to pregnancy and childbirth.   The shocking truth behind these numbers is that half of these can be prevented.   These women are dying because they have no access to health care or maternal care. In fact, 1.3 million women between the ages of 15-44—that's 1 in 5 women of reproductive age—have no health insurance at all.   Many begin pregnancy with untreated or unmanaged conditions that only get worse with pregnancy.

All of these are surely life concerns and should no longer be neglected.

One day I forgot Teddy at daycare. That night, Noah, being too young to understand, cried heartbroken for his Teddy Bear and hearing him I was in anguish.

But I had to think what a small thing this is compared to what some children face.   The thought of Noah going through what these children do is terrible to think about. Children are dying from preventable causes, with no health care, no nutrition, no safe water, and no birth attendants.   Little boy soldiers are forced to carry guns and kill.   If we are for life, what kind of life is this?   Hunger is Afghanistan's biggest killer—greater than violence.   To feed and educate their children, parents surrender their children to the Taliban where they are taught suicide bombing is favored by Allah.   Then that boy grows up and lands in Guantanamo Bay. Where there is no redemption—a place to be tortured and punished for being so wicked as to have been born to poor parents who had no food. *"And fear not them which kill the body, but are not able to kill the soul: but rather fear him*

44

which is able to destroy both soul and body in hell." (Matthew 10:28) Endeavoring to see the whole picture, we don't just observe the end result, but consider how a person came to be at Guantanamo Bay or a suicide bomber. How can we pretend to be so concerned about the unborn, but have no concern for the souls of Guantanamo Bay? They are some mother's son whom she held to her breast. They are all terrorists and deserve to be tortured? That's the redemption Jesus paid for? You've investigated? We have no time for investigation, because we have to spend wasted time seeking to reverse Roe. Many of these prisoners have neither been charged nor tried and some have been acknowledged innocent and sent back—though they were tortured. With such treatment we have threatened our own security and have created terrorists with revenge in their hearts. Please see the research. "If Your Enemy Hunger; What Shall We Do With the Prisoners of Guantanamo?" Behind the Walls of Guantanamo. http://www.shiningriver-sheilah.blogspot. com/2009/10/if-your-enemy-hunger_03.html; http://www. shiningriver-sheilah.blogspot.com/2009/09/behind-walls.html; http://www.shiningriver-sheilah.blogspot.com/2009/08/what-shall-we-do-with-prisoners-of.html

"I was father to the poor and the cause I knew not, I searched out" (Job 29:16).

Where is the Christian outrage about this? We have to drown out all thinking with screams of "Baby Killer" at anyone who thinks beyond the reversal of Roe? Many vital concerns go begging because there is no time to give them attention. It is vital to end this war, which is tearing our country apart, wasting so much time, money, and energy without result or solution and fomenting hate. Causing havoc in our political process and draining our resources, this internal impasse touches us all. In our mistaken focus we are weakening our whole society in neglecting the problems and suffering that need to be addressed.

"There needs to be a public outcry!" *"Glory to God in the Highest and on Earth peace,"* the angels sang. What an opportunity lost to show the love of Christ! " *Love your enemies, bless them that curse you, do good to them that hate you and pray for them that despitefully use you and persecute you.. ." By this shall all people know you are My disciples by the love you have one for another..."* (John 13, Matthew 5) By this qualification, how many disciples does Jesus have? I wonder what our world would be like had we applied these principles after 9/11 along with really helping the birth and lives of mothers and children.? *"The weapons of our warfare are not carnal but are mighty through God to the bringing down of strongholds... for we wrestle not against flesh and blood, but against principalities and powers of darkness..."* (II Corinthians   10; Ephesians 6) "We met the enemy and it was us."

Do we want to stop abortion? Then we must prepare for the babies. Keep hospitals like St. Vincent's open and prepare for the 24/7 care some babies may require. Until we are ready to listen to the audible screams of children, leave Roe alone. Let the unborn return to God and play on the grassy slopes of Paradise, or wait in the Garden of Souls. Is there a Garden of Souls? I don't know. There are things we don't know. My first baby, Lori Leigh, lived only 25 hours. I have three children, but I also had two miscarriages and a tubal pregnancy. Do these pregnancies represent souls without a chance to be born? God knows and I'm sure God has ways of taking care of these things. *"As the heavens are higher than the earth so are His ways than our ways.. ."* (Isaiah 55) Your body is not you—it's the house you dwell in.

One thing we can know for sure. Something that is always right—Love.   My daughter, Rebecca, said long ago as I was writing my first paper about peace for the abortion war. One problem: Love denied. One solution: Love applied. *"Judge not, lest ye be judged...Judge not according to appearance, but judge righteous judgment,"* (Matthew 7, John 7) More love. Less judging.

For decades we have allowed ourselves to remain hostage to this kind of thinking. *"The letter kills, but the Spirit gives life. . . their minds were blinded."* (II Corinthians 3:6) Rigid rule keepers know little of the Spirit of God—they cannot. Jesus said the Spirit is like the wind (John 3). If you put the wind in a box, there is no wind. The Word of God has to be living and breathing and flexible—moment by moment. Just as today, the greatest trouble Jesus had was with religious leaders. He had to tell them that *"the Sabbath was made for man; not man for the Sabbath"* (Mark 2) He also said, *"I thank Thee, Father that Thou hast hid these things from the wise and prudent and revealed them unto babes."* (Matthew 11) The religious leaders of Jesus' day have nothing —or vice versa—on some of the religious leaders of today.

*We are not debating when life begins or disputing the miracle of birth or the sanctity of life for we acknowledge these. The Pro-Choice view leaves itself open to wrong arguments as T.W. Wilson points out in his book, *The Key to Lasting Joy*:

> One of the arguments often used by the so-called pro-choice advocates is that the unborn is only a fetus that represents "potential" life, and that it is not a fully human person until it is viable—that is until it is able to survive outside the womb. Until then, they say, the fetus is only a part of the mother, a group of cells growing inside her with whom she can do as she pleases. Using this criterion, they conclude that he fetus is not a child and until late (at least six months) in a pregnancy, and that abortion is therefore permissible at least up to the point of viability. pp. 142,143

When people say, "A woman's right to choose," immediately Roe opponents say, "A woman's right to choose murder? Her body ends where the child's begins." We hear such words as, "Baby killers." Calling a baby a "fetus" gives the impression one gives too little value to the unborn child. Instead focus (1) on the conditions leading to abortion instead of legislation. Focusing on the needs of the people and root causes is the quickest way to fewer abortions and more wanted conceptions. (2) Focus on the fact that outlawing abortion will not solve the problem or stop abortion. That's all we have to agree upon to end this quagmire. We don't have to get into such questions as to when the soul enters the body, etc. Don't distract by saying, "A woman's right to choose." If people are against abortion, don't seek to persuade them otherwise. Focus together on the above two points. Then everyone's goals and needs are better met.

*There are many wonderful organizations promoting life—here are five:

1. **Walking to Beautiful:**
    In 1974, Dr. Catherine Hamlin and her late husband Reginald established the **Addis Ababa Fistula Hospital in Ethiopia**. She says, "The vaginal fistula from obstructed labor is one of the worst injuries that a woman can ever suffer from. She's been in labor, she's suffered tremendous pain and long, long labor, she's lost her baby—the baby is stillborn in nearly every case. Then she is left with urine and body waste leaking from the vagina. This is a most terrible tragedy for a beautiful young girl. Her life is ruined." When you think of little girls forced to give birth, think of labor for a week to give birth to a still born and then her body leaking urine. . . Is this life? Is this God's will? Please listen to the documentary *Walking to Beautiful*. Your heart will be touched by little girls and women, their bodies too small, too young to be giving birth, with no maternal care and too far from the hospital. See the sweet light on their faces when they are cured and given back their lives.

2. **Central Asia Institute:**
    Greg Mortenson in *Three Cups of Tea* and *Stones into Schools* is another most remarkable story of one man's mission to promote peace, one school at a time, in the wildest parts of Pakistan and Afghanistan. Visualize little girls sitting on benches, their faces happy and eager to learn. Greg Mortenson is supporting life. The title of the first book comes from the belief in these countries that if you sit down and have tea with someone three times, they will be your friend. Our irresolvable differences reveal that we haven't been drinking enough tea with those with whom we think

we differ. If we had tea with them—if we looked out their windows, our perceptions might be enlarged.

3. **Yunus Center:**
   Nobel Peace Prize winner, *Muhammad Yunus* , helps poor people in the right way. He is founder of Grameen Bank, pioneered microcredit, a program that provides poor people—mainly women—with small loans they use to launch businesses and lift their families out of poverty. In the past thirty years, microcredit has spread to every continent and benefited over 100 million families. But Yunus remains unsatisfied. Much more could be done, he believes, if the dynamics of capitalism could be applied to humanity's greatest challenges.

   Now in Creating a World without Poverty, Yunus goes beyond microcredit to pioneer the idea of social business... to tackle social problems from poverty and pollution to inadequate health care and lack of education. This book describes how Yunus—in partnerships with some of the world's most visionary business leaders—has launched the world's first purposely designed social business leaders. From collaborating with Danone to produce affordable, nutritious yogurt for malnourished children in Bangladesh to building eyecare hospitals that will save thousands of poor people from blindness.

   "By giving poor people the power to help themselves, Dr. Yunus has offered them something far more valuable than a plate of food—security in its most fundamental form."—Former President Jimmy Carter

   "Muhammad Yunus is a practical visionary who has improved the lives of millions of people in his native Bangladesh and elsewhere in the world." —Los Angeles Times

   " Yunu's ideas have already had a great impact on the Third World, and...hearing his appeal for a 'poverty-free world' from the source itself can be as stirring as that all-American myth of bootstrap success." —*The Washington Post*. http://www.muhammadyunus.org/Publications/creating-a-world-without-poverty/

4. ChildcareKitgum:

An extraordinary story is that of **Irene Gleeson's** who visited Uganda in 1988 and was touched with the plight of the children there. In 1991, she sold her Sydney beachside home in Australia, said goodbye to her four children and grandchildren and went to the war zone of North Uganda. Here she gathered 50 war traumatized children under a mango tree and began to teach and feed them.

Today in 2010: 10,000 children are given Full Day Care/Schooling/medicine and Feeding in 5 CKS schools.

Now CMK Provides
- Medical and malnourished feeding clinic
- Gloryland Junction AIDS hospice & infant orphanage
- Community Churches
- FM Radio Station
- Cultural Arts Studio
- Water bores

See the story for yourself with the Award winning documentary - *Cinderella Children: The Real Diamonds of Africa—God's Children*

Whenever I picture Irene Gleeson—a lady standing there with food and books and little ones, skinny legs running toward her, hope and wonder on their little faces, I feel like crying and wish all children could have such a lady come. But what is preventing it? How many people have ever heard of Irene Gleeson? However, we hear repeatedly of this abortion war—this false compassion, this consuming battle tying up our resources, shouting "Baby Killer" to those outside their narrow view—the belief that the reversal of Roe is the answer. Again and again abortion is the most heated topic of presidential primaries. All these years and there haven't been enough of us realizing how we have been hijacked? Don't allow yourself to be called "pro-abortion" just because you don't give your attention to reversing Roe.

"There needs to be a public outcry against this travesty." Irene Gleeson is another example of a person promoting life. Think of doing more work like she is doing.

5. **World Vision:**
   Our vision for every child, life in all its fullness;
   Our prayer for every heart, the will to make it so

History: World Vision began with the vision of one man. In 1947, Bob Pierce met Tena Hoelkedoer, a teacher, while on a trip to China. She introduced him to a bttered and abandoned child named White Jade. Unable to care for the child herself, she asked, "What are you going to do about her?" Rev. Pierce gave the woman his last five dollars and agreed to send the same amount each month to help the woman care for the girl.

This encounter was a turning point for Rev. Pierce. He began building an organization dedicated to helping the world's children, and in 1950 World Vision was born. The first child sponsorship programme began three years later in response to the need of hundreds of thousands of orphans at the end of the Korean War.

About us: We are called to serve the neediest people of the earth; to relieve their suffering and to promote the transformation of their wellbeing. We stand in solidarity in a common search for justice. We seek to understand the situation of the poor and work alongside them.

We serve all people regardless of religion, race, ethnicity or gender.

We regard all people as created and loved by God. We give priority to people before money, structure, systems, and other institutional machinery. We act in ways that respect dignity, uniqueness, and intrinsic worth of every person — the poor, the donors, our staff and their families, boards, and volunteers. We celebrate the richness of diversity in human personality, culture and contribution.

From President Richard Stearn's page:
July 26, 2010. World Vision is in the forefront of an unprecedented initiative to focus expertise, political will and money on the crisis of unnecessary deaths of pregnant women, babies and infants. Our Child Health Now campaign encourages a movement dedicated to reducing preventable deaths of women and children and is, itself, part of a concerted global effort.

"Let my heart be broken by the things that break the heart of God."—founder, Bob Pierce

What would our world look like if we all did our part? www.worldvision.org

Telling my grandchildren about the Sponsor a Child program, I took them into the study to look up World Vision. Anabelle, my seven-year-old granddaughter chose a five year old girl from Haiti. Children love to help and their hearts are tender to do so. Idea: For birthday parties instead of so many presents they don't need and just get cast aside, why not collect for wells in Africa, or some other purpose?

All of the above organizations show the power of one person.

As I am finishing this book, there is the news story of the firing of Shirley Sherrod. Her speech to the NAACP was edited by a blogger, Andrew Brietbart to make it sound exactly the opposite of what she was really saying. This video was gleefully put on Fox News and the Secretary of Agriculture also became aware

of it. Uncharacteristic in its haste, the Obama administration-
-actually the Secretary of Agriculture-- fired Mrs. Sherrod
without investigating the false evidence. The distortion of truth is
commonplace and certainly Mrs. Sherrod should not have hastily
been fired. However, one good thing to come out of this is that
had not this administration fired her, most people would still be
in the dark as to the true situation. The media climate is at fault
setting up people for these wrong judgments. How can people
know what they believe or how to vote if they are not given the
truth? *"Death and life are in the power of the tongue"* (Proverbs
18:21).

A new headline: "Judge halts stem-cell research," *The
New York Times*, August 25, 2010, calls it a "huge overreach."
Is there something else someone would like to bring up for
controversy so that we have no time to focus on Darfur, or a
mother in Pakistan with no milk for her newborn or little boy
soldiers or little girls behind brothel windows with numbers on
them for customers to choose—perhaps a mosque in the wrong
place that needs people to move to the middle of the bus for
compromise?
I confess that I cannot conjure up the same compassion for
an embryonic stem cell in the same way I do when I see the face
of a mother who has no food for her children.

However, we no longer are held hostage, for the sword
of truth has revealed this taunting Goliath to be in actuality the
"Baby Killer" itself consuming our center of attention instead of
preparing for healing and restoration and an environment of love
and safety for children.

Stop!

Go no further!

Turn around!

"Turn!

Turn!

Turn!"

It's past time for truth to put its boots on. We no longer allow our legislative process to be hijacked by this so-called "Pro-Life" mentality which is really "Pro-Death" doing more harm than good, sapping us of our vitality, polarizing and distracting us from crucial duties and needs, sucking the life out of our democracy and helping noone, least of all the unborn. What kind of an environment are we preparing for children? With eyes open we no longer tolerate the drowning of our voices by hypocritical madness yelling "baby killer" hanging in effigy, consigning to hell. I, for one, respect the sanctity of life-- love the verses in Psalm 139—I am in wonder at the miracle of giving birth—people like us should not arbitrarily be called" pro-abortion" or "baby killers" just because we realize the wisdom of working with root causes instead of the reversal of Roe. The extreme elements out there that have been hijacking our legislative process need to be depleted of energy. As Nicholas Kristoff says in his article, "Sister Margaret's Choice," *New York Times*, "There needs to be a public outcry." What kind of thinking consigns a little 79 pounds nine year old girl, pregnant by the rape of her stepfather, to continue and endure the pregnancy? What kind of thinking ex-communicates a nun like Sister Margaret for saving the life of a mother when both mother and child would have died? No wonder some people say they are atheists. They reject the god that has been presented to them. Every situation, every pregnancy is unique. We are the people who investigate and listen and pray and walk in the woods. We don't allow ourselves to get into destructive mob mentality crucifying the life out of our democracy. If this same energy and passion that has been given to the organizing of protests and trying to reverse Roe, had been directed to real solutions and relieving suffering, we could be having utopia by now.

We wish for our brother's and sister's children what we wish for our own children. It all goes together. As I help the

54

children of the world, I help my own. We love children and want the best for every precious baby.

"Let my heart be broken by the things that break the heart of God."—Bob Pierce, founder of World Vision

What would our world look like if we all did our part?

We visualize it and do God's work God's way. We leave Roe alone. This fruitless argument is rather like arguing about whether to clip the hedge or let it grow free when there is a bulldozer down the road apace that will mow the whole thing down, clipped or free. We focus together on the bulldozer. We have a President who knows what to do regarding the abortion issue. There are plenty of projects to put our hands to. The terms: Pro-Life, Pro-Choice, Pro-Abortion, Anti-Abortion are history-laden. We throw them in the river with a "No Fishing" sign. We are full of LIFE! No more distractions, no more name-calling, no more-excessive-time-and-money- campaigns! The Life of our democracy depends upon it! We are for Life—these are Life issues. We are Americans, and with God's help, we are equal to the task! God is *"plenteous in redemption"* (Psalm 130). We allow ourselves to be redeemed!

We are

La Verde de la Vida!

...a thrill of hope,

the weary world rejoices

for yonder breaks a new and glorious morn

Stand on your feet, O hear the angel voices...

Will you be a part of: *La Verde de la Vida*?

Our declaration:

I accept *La Verde de la Vida*. Knowing that the reversal of Roe not only provides no answers, but actually prevents solutions, I support real efforts to reduce abortion and promote life, such as: clean water, nutrition, health care, maternal pregnancy care, adoption, an end to child soldiers, and child sex trafficking. We do not support the manipulation of our society by this unproductive single issue focus on the reversal of Roe. We are *La Verde de la Vida*.

"And the streets of the city shall be full of boys and girls playing..." (Zechariah 8:5)

After President Clinton's Second Inaugural Address, a reporter, when asked if he thought he heard anything really quotable --I suppose like, "Ask not what your country can do for you, but what you can do for your country."-- said, "No, I don't think so." However, I did:

"The greatest progress needs to be made in the human heart."
--President William Jefferson Clinton

Cadenza

The Civil War

The abortion war is said to be the issue that won't go away—as divisive as slavery before the Civil War.

George Washington had a dream at Valley Forge in which he saw a vision of three times of trouble for America—the Revolutionary War, the Civil War and the worst to come. However, prophesy and prophetic dreams do not have to come to pass. They are a warning of what the prophetic eye sees if present circumstances do not change.

What is in the world? It is a picture of what is in each of our hearts. Inasmuch as we listen to our hearts and do our part—inasmuch as we go by The Golden Rule (or don't go by The Golden Rule), we are responsible for the violence or the peace in this world.

Shelby Foote (1916-2005) wrote a massive three volume history of the Civil War. This was used for a PBS documentary by Ken Burns. When I saw the film, I couldn't get it out of my mind. I kept thinking about how important it is to learn from this war for present-day problems.

Did we have to have the Civil War? Some may think we did—to free the slaves, to preserve the union. After the Civil War was supposedly over, however, the terrible conflict continued, so much so that it was called the Second Civil War. Hearts were not changed—in fact, hatred had multiplied and for many ex-slaves conditions were even worse. There was the so called Jim Crow legislation passed by the southern states as soon as they joined the union, which made racial inequality laws. Lynching was common place and the outlawing of it couldn't even get through the Senate. Dr. Martin Luther King and the freedom marches haven't been so far in the distant past. Mississippi just recently had the trial and conviction of the man who orchestrated the death of three Civil Rights leaders.

I wish there could be a PBS documentary about John Woolman of the Quakers. We hear much of John Brown and his bloody methods, but what about John Woolman? I talk of him often—most of the time people have never heard of him. He

(1720-1772) was an example of the right way to change wrong. (Notice his dates-- over a hundred years before the Civil War.)

John Woolman was convinced that slavery was wrong and so he went from Quaker meeting to Quaker meeting preaching this message. He actually traveled on foot from New England to North Carolina. In 1758, he convinced the Philadelphia Quakers at their yearly meeting to give up slavery—imagine that! We should have a national holiday about this! Hearts were changed. These were permanent results. Would that John Woolman's message had been taken up by others and the Civil War averted. (Later the Quakers were at the forefront of the Underground Railroad.)

Redemption-- from The President's Easter Prayer Breakfast

"....One of my hopes upon taking this office was to make the White House a place where all people would feel welcome. To that end, we held a Seder here to mark the first Passover. We held an Iftar here with Muslim Americans to break the daily fast during Ramadan. And today, I'm particularly blessed to welcome you, my brothers and sisters in Christ, for this Easter breakfast... I wanted to join you for a brief moment today to continue the Easter celebration of our risen Savior, and to reflect on the work to which His promise calls all of us.

"I can't tell any of you anything about Easter that you don't already know. (Laughter.) I can't shed light on centuries of scriptural interpretation or bring any new understandings to those of you who reflect on Easter's meaning each and every year and each and every day. But what I can do is tell you what draws me to this holy day and what lesson I take from Christ's sacrifice and what inspires me about the story of the resurrection.

"For even after the passage of 2,000 years, we can still picture the moment in our mind's eye. The young man from Nazareth marched through Jerusalem; object of scorn and derision and abuse and torture by an empire. The agony of crucifixion amid the cries of thieves. The discovery, just three days later, that would forever alter our world -- that the Son of Man was not to be found in His tomb and that Jesus Christ had risen.

"We are awed by the grace He showed even to those who would have killed Him. We are thankful for the sacrifice He gave for the sins of humanity. And we glory in the promise of redemption in the resurrection.

And such a promise is one of life's great blessings, because, as I am continually learning, we are, each of us, imperfect. Each of us errs -- by accident or by design. Each of us falls short of how we ought to live. And selfishness and pride are vices that afflict us all.

"It's not easy to purge these afflictions, to achieve

redemption. But as Christians, we believe that redemption can be delivered -- by faith in Jesus Christ. And the possibility of redemption can make straight the crookedness of a character; make whole the incompleteness of a soul. redemption makes life, however fleeting here on Earth, resound with eternal hope.

"Of all the stories passed down through the gospels, this one in particular speaks to me during this season. And I think of hanging -- watching Christ hang from the cross, enduring the final seconds of His passion. He summoned what remained of His strength to utter a few last words before He breathed His last breath.

"Father," He said, *"into your hands I commit my spirit."* Father, into your hands I commit my spirit. These words were spoken by our Lord and Savior, but they can just as truly be spoken by every one of us here today. Their meaning can just as truly be lived out by all of God's children.

"So, on this day, let us commit our spirit to the pursuit of a life that is true, to act justly and to love mercy and walk humbly with the Lord. And when we falter, as we will, let redemption -- through commitment and through perseverance and through faith -- be our abiding hope and fervent prayer..."
-Barak Obama

The President modestly says that he doesn't expect to tell them anything they haven't heard before or give any new interpretation of this scripture. And yet, for me--I who have been listening to Easter sermons since before I was born--my mother taking me to church--found something in this message especially deep and new affecting me I think as no other Easter message has. Perhaps the timing and the soil of my heart and my concerns. I thought, what if we as a country really believed in redemption? How would it affect our prison system? (We incarcerate more people than any other developed country.) What about Guantanamo Bay? If a person believed in redemption, could they ever think that torture is the means of keeping us safe? Some deride the fact of "lawyers being used for terrorists" --never mind these people haven't even been tried so how can you know if they are innocent or guilty.

As I ran over to Van Cortlandt Park to pray, it came to me, "Jesus is a lawyer for terrorists." What about the Apostle Paul? If we are truly followers of the Christ—if we believe in the work of Jesus on the cross—if we embrace the message of the resurrection, then we must believe in redemption.

It's the answer to terrorism. May our eyes be open to this revelation. We need resurrection. Our country needs redemption. Let's allow ourselves to be redeemed. Let's open our hearts to receive it.

Rwanda

Coming from babysitting my grandson, Noah, I walked in late and took a seat on the back row of the West End Collegiate Church here in New York City. Immaculee Ilibagiza, a survivor of the Rwandan Genocide, was speaking. Her book, *Left Behind Discovering God Amidst the Rwandan Holocaust* (2006), is an autobiographical work detailing how she survived during the Rwandan Genocide. She was featured on PBS on one of Wayne Dyer's programs, and also on a December 3, 2006 segment of 60 Minutes (which re-aired on July 1, 2007).

Left to Tell recounts how Immaculée Ilibagiza survived for 91 days with seven other women during the holocaust in a damp and small bathroom, no larger than 3 feet long and 4 feet (1.2m) wide. Immaculee speaks all over the world and is the recipient of the 2007 Mahatma Gandhi Reconciliation and Peace Award.,

This book, along with *Led by Faith*, and *Our Lady of Kibeho*, are on the *New York Times* best seller list

From *Publisher's Weekly*:

This searing firsthand account cuts two ways: her description of the evil that was perpetrated, including the brutal murders of her family members is soul-numbingly devastating, yet the story of her unquenchable faith and connection to God throughout the ordeal uplifts and inspires. This book is a precious addition to the literature that tries to make sense of humankind' seemingly bottomless depravity and counterbalancing hope in an all-powerful, loving God.

At once the speaker's voice arrested me—I felt God's presence. And later, as I saw her up close, I noticed how beautiful she was—her face had the quiet radiance of someone who has spent much time in prayer. Her communion with God enabled her to have victory over unforgiveness and grief.

Being reminded of the Rwandan genocide, I realized all the more the importance of resolving our conflicts in such a way as to not tear our country apart. Could we not release unnecessary pressure for our elected leaders by praying for them and looking for the things they do that are good instead of being so quick to criticize and revel at every seeming misstatement?. In our elections, isn't there much digging into the past rejoicing to find something against an opponent? Do we know what happened between that person and God even yesterday? Our prison system—are there not many wrong judgments and a lack of belief in redemption?

At the church I saw these two quotations:

"With malice toward none and charity toward all..."
--Abraham Lincoln

Our diversity unites us.

In realizing our nation, our world, individually and collectively, faces challenges and perils too vast for human strength, what can we do? We must enlist the heavenly host—going beyond what we see and hear. (I love the story found in II Kings 6: 8-23which illustrates angelic help and also gives an example of, "*If your enemy hunger, feed him.*") We must stop eating from the tree of the knowledge of good and evil (which is still a tree of death), jumping to judgment, but must be quiet in our spirits waiting for the discernment and wisdom from "*The One Who Inhabits Eternity.*"

Judge not according to appearance, but judge righteous judgment. (John 7:24)

Situations can be so different from what they appear to be. Judging "*according to appearance*" is judging with human understanding alone; judging "*righteous judgment*" is judging with the discernment that God gives which is available to everyone if they will listen. Our Father/Mother "*delights in mercy*" and is "*plenteous in redemption*"; if we would be representatives of the divine, we must let mercy, love and redemption flow through us.

As we begin this New Year with a new administration, may

we deal with our differences as assets to enlarge our perceptions and not as liabilities to divide us.

The climate of hatred proceeded the genocide.

from *Left to Tell*:
I was born in paradise.

At least, that's how I felt about my homeland while I was growing up.

Rwanda is a tiny country set like a jewel in central Africa. She is so breathtakingly beautiful that it's impossible not see the hand of God in her lush, rolling hills; mist-shrouded mountains; green valley; and sparkling lakes. The gentle breezes drifting down from the hills and through the pine and cedar forests are scented with the sweet aroma of lilies and chrysanthemums. . .

The forces of evil that would give birth to a holocaust that set my beloved country awash in a sea of blood were hidden from me as a child. As a young girl all I knew of the world was the lovely landscape surrounding me, the kindness of my neighbors, and the deep love of my parents and brothers. In our home, racism and prejudice were completely unknown...

In my village, young children walked eight miles to and from school along lonely stretches of road, but parents never worried about a child being abducted or harmed in any way...

from *Led by Faith*:
It wasn't' until I was well into my schooling that I realized our parents had protected my brothers and me... We were never told about the ugly prejudiced, simmering ethnic tensions, and hate-mongering politics that had been driving our compatriots apart, which ultimately laid the groundwork for one of history's bloodiest

genocides...

By April 1994, the fuel for genocide had been gathered and prepared, and it was ready to be ignited. . . President Habyarimana was killed when his plane was shot down during the night while returning from peace talks. Within the hour, Hutu extremists set their carefully laid plans for genocide in motion. The killing started immediately..."

Tragedy is the result of being distracted from matters left unattended. *"Buy the truth and sell it not; also wisdom, instruction and knowledge"* (Proverbs 23:23)" The longer we wait to stand for truth the greater will be the price when you finally –or are forced to– stand. World War I and World War II are examples—as well as other wars—when the cup of iniquity is full and has to topple over.

Some say to God, "How could you let this happen?" We are co-creators with God—He has chosen to work through flesh and blood, giving us free will to serve Him or not to serve Him— to be hands, feet and voice through which He speaks or not to do so. And God would say, "How could you let this happen?" God is love, and *"He is not willing that any should perish."* It can be one minute to midnight until everything blows up, but if enough people—

> *"If My People who are called by My name, shall humble themselves and pray, And seek My face, and turn from their wicked ways, Then will I hear from heaven, And will forgive their sin, And will heal their land."* (II Chronicles 7:14)

> *"And I sought for a man among them that should make up the hedge, and stand in the gap before me for the land, that I should not destroy it..."* (Ezekiel 22:30) (Actually we do it to ourselves.)

Will you determine to be that one man—that one woman—if enough people, realize the power of one—think what *a mighty stream...*

Who knows how many one-minute-till-midnight-moments we have had in America and in history? And somewhere someone, enough people connected to the Invisible Host. (http://shiningriver-sheilah.blogspot.com/2009/10/if-your-enemy-hunger_03.html) and time, so to speak, was pushed back to 9:00 to give more people a chance to understand.

Think and those people could push —

Oh, let justice roll as a mighty stream—*"let judgment run down as waters, and righteousness as a mighty stream."* (Amos 5:24)—

back 24 hours, back a week, a year. The Prophetic eye sees in the spirit world— what will manifest in the physical if the *status quo* remains the same. But prophecy is moving—it goes up and down depending who is obeying and listening. (Jeremiah 18:1-10).

"The earth groans and travails... until the manifestation of the sons and daughters of God." (Romans 8)

It does not take a prophetic eye to see that our world stands on the brink of total annihilation. Did you ever consider that our thoughts can cause global warming; and conversely, the reverse? The Greatest Tribulation the world has ever known? Surely, this prophecy can be visualized without any prophetic voice. What about pushing time back and back and back and back and push The Greatest Tribulation the world has ever known off of the edge of eternity? To say The Greatest Tribulation is behind us—what about that? PBS in the World War II document said it was the greatest destruction the world has ever known. Let's say, enough tribulation. Let's qualify for:

"Glory to God in the Highest and on earth peace..." (Luke 2).

"The wolf shall dwell with the lamb…a little child shall lead… they shall beat their swords into plowshares and not learn war anymore."(Isaiah 2:11; Micah 4)

"And such as do wickedly against the covenant shall be corrupt by flatteries: but the people that do know their God shall be strong, and do exploits… And they that be wise shall shine as the brightness of the firmament; and they that turn many to righteousness as the stars for ever and ever." (Daniel 11:32; 12:3)

Prayer for our President and Nation

Lord, we pray that you arise in our nation, our media, in our leaders--that all that is not of you be scattered. May blind eyes be open and deaf ears unstopped to your voice. You are the Prince of Peace. We know *"we do not wrestle against flesh and blood but against principalities and powers of darkness and spiritual wickedness in high places."*

We pray especially for our young President. He has been given problems beyond human ability to solve. We acknowledge our part in causing our nation to be in this present situation. We repent and acknowledge that *unless you build the nation we labor in vain*--no matter what wonderful plans we think we have. Cause our President to call upon You continually for wisdom and guidance. We know these problems are very small--as grasshoppers in Your sight. You can turn things around in a moment when our hearts and consciousness are right. *Still the enemy and the avenger,* pour oil on the angry spirits so that your Spirit come forth taking those off of the media to make room for those who should be on. *Let the words of our mouth and the meditation of our hearts be acceptable to you.* Let your voice be heard! Let it be heard through us!

"But the mouth of them that speak lies shall be stopped..." (Psalm 63:11)

"O Thou that hearest prayer unto Thee shall all flesh come. Inquities prevail against me: as for our transgressions, Thou shalt purge them away. Blessed is the woman whom Thou choosest, and causest to approach unto Thee, that she may dwell in Thy court: we shall be satisfied with the goodness of Thy house, even of Thy holy temple." (Psalm 65:2-4)

"He ruleth by His power forever; His eyes behold the nations: let not the rebellious exalt themselves. Selah"

"O bless our God, ye people, and make The Voice of His praise to be heard."

"We went through fire and through water: but Thou broughtest us out into a wealthy place."

"Come and hear, all ye that fear God, and I will declare what He hath done for my soul."

The Mosque—A Defining Moment

As a Christian, I believe in redemption. As an American, I believe in religious liberty. Roger Williams, founder of Rhode Island said, "Faith by its very nature must be a free act." Though a Baptist and strong in his faith, he did not exclude people from Rhode Island because of their religion or even no religion. He said that government should be concerned about law and order, not religious belief. It was foundational for our religious liberty and should be an example for us today.

The label does not determine what something (or somebody) is. Many horrible things have been done in the name of religion--would I want to be held accountable for what some, who have the label of "Christian", have done? Not all people who say they are "Christian" are peacemakers and follow the teachings of Jesus: *"But I say unto you, Love your enemies, bless them that curse you, do good to them that hate you, and pray for them which despitefully use you, and persecute you; That ye may be the children of your Father which is in heaven . . .Blessed are the peacemakers."* (Matthew 5)

Likewise not all Muslims are terrorists and it is unfair and un-American and a betrayal of our values to make them accountable or exclude them because of what some Muslims have done--it is insensitive in the extreme.

Muslims were also killed on 9/11. Listen to your heart; have some empathy. Think of how some of them must feel. I don't want them to think this is Christianity. Do we want to be

72

known as a culture of vengeance? Or have the barbaric belief in collective guilt and collective punishment? What if we believed in redemption? Isn't that foundational to what Christians believe along with forgiveness, grace and mercy? *"Forgive us our trespasses as we forgive those who trespass against us."* (John 13). Jesus said, *"By this shall all people know you are my disciples if you have love one for another."* By this qualification, how many disciples does Jesus have? To allow this cultural center and mosque does not mean compromising what we believe or a blurring of the significant differences between our religions. To forbid it compromises our American values. I'm grateful for the speeches of both the Mayor of New York and the President of the United States--neither of which need retract anything. As a matter of principle, that mosque cannot be relocated out of fear. No one need move to the middle of the bus.

Clearly there are those who want to stir up faith based opposition for their political opponents. Among those against the New York mosque are the very vocal Newt Gingrich and Sarah Palin. However, in opposition to this view, President Obama reminds us at a Whitehouse speech for Ramadan: http://www.whitehouse.gov/the-press-office/2010/08/13/remarks-president-iftar-dinner-0 "This is America. And our commitment to religious freedom must be unshakeable. The principle that people of all faiths are welcome to this country and that they will not be treated differently by their government is essential to who we are. The writ of the Founders must endure."

Matters of religious liberty should have been settled long ago—in fact, they were.

And Newt Gingrich, you're trying to take this away from us—and as a potential political candidate? Your efforts would be better served and the cause of peace by helping the children and people of Pakistan's flood, instead of forcing our focus on forbidding mosques.

Despite abundant evidence to the contrary, (For example, PBS, October 10, 2008, "Religion and Ethics: What the Candidates Believe," "All four candidates describe themselves as Christian... Barak Obama has been the most outspoken about matters of faith..." [says Obama], 'I believe that Jesus Christ died for my sins and that I am redeemed through him. That is a source of strength and sustenance on a daily basis. I know that I don't walk alone.'" http://www.pbs.org/wnet/religionandethics/episoes/october-10-2008-campaign-what-the-candidates-believe/885/). There are voices that wish to portray the President as "secular" or Muslim. It is said that one out of five Americans wrongly believe this. And now the Iftar speech is eagerly given as evidence to perpetuate this claim. Mr. Gingrich helps fuel this confusion. Take his book title: *Stop the Secular, Socialist Obama Machine*. What needs to be stopped is how Mr. Gingrich invents things. A very provable invention is that Mr. Gingrich, promoting his writer, Vince Halley, accused the President of" "editing Jesus out of Easter." (http://www.torenewamerica.com/obama-removes-jesus-from-easter-message)

From this accusation came at least three googled pages of outrage against the President—and who knows how much on talk radio and TV. Talk about a machine, Mr. Gingrich, your polarizing, hostility machine needs to be stopped and NOW! And we're to consider you an example of spirituality? Jesus speaks of *"the wheat and the tares"* growing together. It seems the tares often get the microphone. This is unacceptable. Truth and love shall arise and come forth and their voices shall swallow up and scatter that which is not.

"Strive not with a man without cause, if he have done thee no harm." (Proverbs 3:30)

Yes, Sarah, there is a death panel. *"Death and Life are in the power of the tongue"* (Proverbs 18:21) Your death panel statement was like an avalanche which brought unreasonable anger against our President and our government. People couldn't even talk in the town meetings. We have to listen to one another. Sarah, people who trust in you--who like your sparkling vivaciousness--believe you. For good debate and solutions, it is important that the truth be known and you are the person who has the stage to tell it. Do you agree? Especially when you know many are listening and some are ready to follow your example, it is totally irresponsible to falsely accuse the President of something "downright evil." This is abusive power of your freedom of speech and democracy can't work this way. Before such a drastic statement is made--before one pours kerosene on differences, there is a need to double check and get facts straight. I cannot express myself too strongly. Extreme harm has been done, and I feel you need to apologize to the President and to the American people and publicly explain since you so publicly accused.

"*Do violence to no man, neither accuse any falsely...*" (Luke 3:14). Your "Death Panels" lie was given the Lie of the Year award by *St. Petersburg Times*, home of *The Politifact*, which was awarded the 2009 Pulitzer Prize in Journalism. However, unfortunately, some people don't know it was a lie. (For fuller explanation see: http://shiningriver-sheilah.blogspot.com/2010/07/dear-sarah-to-begin-these-words-from.html) Talk about Mama Grizzles, I'm enlisting. It certainly is true that lies circle the globe while truth is just getting its boots on.

Getting our boots on, President Obama gave two Easter messages—neither of which he "edited" Jesus out. (In one he did not quote everything another speaker said.) Instead Mr. Gingrich is the one doing the editing. This is a serious accusation clearly designed to stir up the people. Take Jesus and the resurrection out of Easter which is most precious to Christians? Please listen to the President's Easter Prayer Breakfast Message –he speaks of redemption. I have listened to it ten times and took it to church for others to listen to: We need redemption. Who dares judge the President "secular"? (http://www.whitehouse.gov/photos-and-video/video/white-house-easter-prayer-breakfast)

"*But the King (the President) shall rejoice in God. . .but the mouth of them that speak lies shall be stopped.*" (Psalm 63:11)

At the prayer breakfast the President said of Jesus, "We are awed by the grace He showed even to those who would have killed Him. We are thankful for the sacrifice He gave for the sins of humanity. And we glory in the promise of redemption in the resurrection."

I am awed by the grace of the President. In all my years—I

have three children and seven grandchildren so I am not young—I have never known anyone to be criticized so unfairly who so little deserves it. He is not perfect, I do not agree with all policies, but he "is trying hard," as he said, "and wants the best for our country." Who are the perfect ones to throw stones? If you don't like the polices, I'm sure he could do better without all this edit-Jesus-out-of-Easter kind of criticism. And who knows—with all this commotion—what some of the policies really are? If he has made unwise decisions and you've been fault finding and seeing what you can dig up and take out of context, then you're part of the problem. Do you make good decisions when you are being constantly criticized and lies are being thrown about? I have never before realized how much our collective consciousness limits the options and decisions of those in Washington. We are to pray for our leaders. As a friend said, "The Bible says to pray without ceasing. Where does it say to criticize without ceasing?" What if we got the President some say we have? There needs to be some gratitude. Two quotations from college days: 1) "Constructive suggestions welcome; gripping not tolerated." 2) "When gratitude dies on the altar of a man's [nation's] heart, he is well nigh hopeless." We need to nourish and uplift our young President. What kind of hearts do we have? I feel like crying. To combat all this negative energy, I'm going to praise the President:

for his love of country and people,

for his knowledge and intelligence--

that he has diligently studied our history, our founders, and our Constitution,

that he is appreciative of our diversity of cultures,

that he stays calm under pressure, (In this culture, this is BIG one. ("*He that is slow to anger is better than the mighty; and he that ruleth his spirit than he that taketh a city.*" Proverbs 16:32) that he is a listener--that he wants to hear and consider opposing views and that he wants to be fair,

for his wisdom and speaking ability,

that he is forgiving and not vengeful, for his generous spirit,

that he knows, as he has expressed, the importance of humility,

for his sense of humor.

I'm thankful for how noble he is and that we can be proud of him when he travels to other countries and gives speeches.

I'm thankful for his dignity.

I'm thankful for his family--for Michelle and his girls to whom he is a good husband and father.

I'm thankful that he is a man of faith,

A man named Bill Derksen, apparently from another country, in responding to PBS analysis expressed, "...it is increasingly clear that journalists absolutely MUST criticize a president at all cost to maintain 'credibility'. My perception of your president is that he is one of the greatest leaders of all time, appreciated in almost all other countries, and perhaps, the most under appreciated, under supported president in your own country..."

And now the climate of our country has escalated in controversy over the dream project of another leader, Imam Feisal Rauf. Who is he? A biographical sketch is given in "Complicated Balancing Act For Imam in Mosque Furor," *New York Times*, August 22, 2010 When giving a speech in Cairo in February, the imam said, "Muslims need to understand and soothe Americans who fear them. They should be conciliatory, not judgmental, toward the West and Israel." He was asked, "Aren't you being financed by the United States?" "I'm not an agent from any government," he said, "I'm a peacemaker." . . . Akbar Ahmed, professor of Islamic studies says, "He hurtles in, to the dead-center eye of the storm. . .expecting it to be like at his mosque--we all love each other, we all think happy thoughts. . .so this mild-mannered guy is in the eye of a storm for which he's not suited at all."

I disagree. He is well suited. In the eye of the storm is silence, peace. This is especially needed in this chaos. I'm grateful. We need this calm. We've enough fanatical voices and the last thing we need is more hothead leaders. I'm grateful that our President keeps his cool--he's an example for us--for me. But even for this, he is criticized. Consider:

"He that is slow to anger is better than the mighty; and he that ruleth his spirit than he that taketh a city." (Proverbs 16:32)

"An ungodly man diggeth up evil: and in his lips there is as a burning fire." (Proverbs 16:27)

Perhaps you, like me, have found that often you have more rapport with those under another label than with those supposedly under your own label. Lesson: Forget labels. Remember love. *Sojourners* has a civility pledge. The Coffee Party has a civility pledge. Americans are longing for civility. We are tired of this "endless spewing" of which the oil spill was a metaphor.

In "Obama and the Chaos Perception," *New York Times,* June 6, 2010, Matt. Bai states that since President Obama is a gifted writer, he will "understand the power of a good metaphor... the poetic significance of that cloud of oil... spewing endlessly... the accumulating cloud..."

Yes, the accumulating cloud .
Spewing endlessly.

As has been said in many ways by poets, mystics, and theologians, both ancient and modern: The physical is a shadow of the reality in the spirit. The president should appreciate the poetic significance? I disagree with the author's metaphor. What about we as a people appreciating the poetic significance?

What accumulating cloud has been spewing endlessly? Criticism, the distortion of truth, jumping to judgment. The birthers saying the President was born in Ghana and so is disqualified to be president, Glenn Beck Rush Limbaugh and other T.V. and radio hosts leading a mentality comparing the President to Hitler, Stalin, and calling him a communist or a Nazi. Ann Coulter referring to the President as "B. Hussein Obama" in a derogatory way--his middle name should be an asset to connecting with Muslims. He is criticized even for giving a speech to the school children about working hard and staying in school--some advised boycotting that school day. We're supposed to turn liabilities into assets-- not assets into liabilities. What a role model and inspiration for our black youth--all of our youth. The fact that he is both black and white should be another asset. Fortunately, others, including Laura Bush, praised him and defended his back-to-school speech, but damage was certainly done. Oh, why can't we pull together and be proud of our President, The First Lady and the children? There's Michelle, she looks like so much fun--the smile on her face, a lady of style and I love her thinking up a vegetable garden for the Whitehouse. I am positive there is nothing we can't do if we stop this negativity and help one another--Listen to your heart and do your part!

There is no greater threat to our democracy than this endless spewing. This accumulating cloud hangs now over ground zero.

When my children were young and quarreling, I sometimes put them on "silence." Like unruly children, there are those who need to be put on silence--Newt Gingrich, you're on silence, as well as Sarah Palin, Rush Limbaugh, Glenn Beck, Ann Coulter, Keith Halloran, others—on the left as well as the right—put your name in there--Actually, we all need to do this--have moments of silence. Go for a walk in the woods, pray, meditate, let the Spirit speak to you--through the birds, the rippling of the water, the whispering of the leaves. Get away from *The Maddening Crowd*, have a Walden moment, get a John Muir complex--most of all walk with the Master and sit, as Mary, at His feet. He is the

Prince of Peace. "*I come to the garden alone, while the dew is still on the roses…*"

This is the best way to affect what happens in Washington, our country, our world. (http://shiningriver-sheilah.blogspot.com/2009/10/if-your-enemy-hunger_03.html)

Read a chapter out of Proverbs everyday. There are 31 chapters so read whatever day it is and then start over. Wisdom needs to arise and craziness needs to fall. "*Wisdom crieth without; she uttereth her voice in the streets.*" (Proverbs 1:20) We need to build up our reservoir of wisdom. Actually I believe it's out there, but outrageous voices have been competing and almost drowning it out. America has all the wisdom, information, understanding, gifts, talents and abilities to do everything in this country that needs doing and answer every problem that needs solving. We have so many wonderful, kind-hearted, generous people, but it's hard to hear them. And with these political campaigns-with millions of dollars being spent –actually much to finance this spewing--words that should not be said--think of, not only, the money, but the time spent on elections. How can we get anything done? Did you see the pictures of the children in the flooding of Pakistan? Mothers giving birth and no milk? It *tears* at my heart. What if that were my two-year-old grandson, Noah? What if this campaign money was sent to Pakistan? I pray we have politicians who say, "I'm getting off this train." I'm going to take a walk in the woods. I'm going to trust and have the backing of the "*One Who inhabits eternity*".

We need to know our seasons—when to speak and when to be silent. When to take center stage and when to retreat backstage. Too many people have been in the spotlight too long who should be going to the back side of the desert.

I need the silence and have been as though in labor going almost daily to Van Cortlandt Urban Forest near me. Today's verses:

"*Go not forth hastily to strive, lest thou know not what to do in the end thereof, when thy neighbour hath put thee to shame. . . A word fitly spoken is like apples of gold in pictures of silver. As an earring of gold, and an ornament of fine gold, so is a wise reprover upon an obedient ear.*" (Proverbs 25)

This is really a teaching opportunity and defining moment for us as Americans. Who are we and what do we believe? What positions do we take and why? Other countries are watching. I am embarrassed over these protestors. Some Arab countries do not allow churches. Is this an example for us, or are we the example? I pray that many will rethink this matter and follow the leadership of our President and come to wisdom and understanding regarding it and let it be an opening for healing, beauty and restoration--and thus the sacrifice of those who died there and since then be memorialized, the ground hallowed.

> "What better could be done with an enemy than to make him a friend, and especially to make him a friend of God… It enables you to see unlimited possibilities in everyone and even in the most tragic of situations"—J. Rufus Moseley

Notes:
Rev. Jim Wallis of Sojourners writes in his article, "Who Wins When the U.S. Restricts Religious Freedom?" "When Muslim leaders step up to lead an initiative to reduce tensions and promote respect and understanding, do we first judge those leaders by the actions of terrorists… Feisal Rauf and his wife Daisy Khan are friends of mine, and I can testify that they are indeed peacemakers."

On NPR, August 25, 2010 I was directed to Iman Rauf's words on 60 Minutes: Below are some quotes—not all of which were referred to on NPR, Brian Leher: Invoking Pearl's final words before his beheading, Rauf declared: "If to be a Jew means to say with all one's heart, mind and soul, 'Sh'ma Yisrael Adonai Elohenu Adonai Ehad -- hear O Israel, the Lord our God, the Lord is One,' not only today I am a Jew, I have always been one.'"

The critics come armed with their own set of quotes: Shortly after the September 11, 2001 attacks, the imam told "60 Minutes" that

"I wouldn't say that the United States deserved what happened; but the United States policies were an accessory to the crime that happened." In a radio interview in June with WABC's Aaron Klein, Rauf described himself as a "supporter of Israel," but declined to label Hamas as a terrorist group, saying, "I do not want to be placed nor will I accept a position where I am the target of one side or another." And, this week, his detractors are trumpeting a 2005 speech in Adelaide, Australia, in which he cited the impact of U.S.-led sanctions on Iraq and asserted that "we tend to forget, in the West, that the United States has more Muslim blood on its hands than Al Qaeda has on its hands of innocent non-Muslims." The quote discussed on NPR and said by some to be under attack was:

"I wouldn't say that the United States deserved what happened; but the United States policies were an accessory to the crime that happened."

My friends, that sounds like the word of the Lord. Jesus said, "*My sheep hear My voice and another they will not follow.*" "*If any speak, let her (let him) speak as the oracles of God*" (I Peter). We can hear the voice of Jesus through the words of another. Are there those who object to the Imam statement? We are a perfect nation and have nothing for which to repent? I think not. When I heard the President's speech in Cairo, I heard greatness—no wonder the people of Norway were so affected. Those voices who criticize the President's apologies on our behalf as a nation definitely need to take a walk in the woods. It needs to become a cliché—have you walked in the woods? Before you speak or write a book—have you taken a walk in the woods? I need the silence—I ask myself, have I gone to Van Cortlandt Park, so to speak—have I spent time in the quiet place, the Secret Place?

We do not condone violence for any reason. For we know "*that the weapons of our warfare are not carnal, but mighty through God to the pulling down of strongholds... for we wrestle not against flesh and blood, but against principalities and powers of darkness and spiritual wickedness in high places.*"

However, we reflect upon 9/11 and ask the Spirit to show us. How did it happen? What door was left open? What shall we do differently? What shall we do for our safety and the safety of our children? We need to see behind the scenes. We cannot listen to those who grab statements—the twisters, causing verbal hurricanes and tornadoes. We are ready to repent and ask forgiveness. Thank God for a President who knows this

A quote from *The Audacity of Hope*, by President Obama:

> "No, what's troubling is the gap between the magnitude of our challenges and the smallness of our politics—the ease with which we are distracted by the petty and trivial, our chronic avoidance of tough decisions, our seeming inability to build a working consensus to tackle any big problem..." p.22

The answer is still:

> "*If my people, who are called by my name shall humble themselves and pray, and seek my face, and turn from their wicked ways; then will I hear from heaven, and will forgive their sin, and will heal their land.*" (II Chronicles 7:14)

Answering: How did 9/11 affect you?

SECURITY IS IN THE SECRET PLACE

I live in Riverdale in the Bronx, less than one hour by subway from the World Trade Center. The morning of 9/11 I went to vote. I half heard some ladies talking something about, "Isn't it terrible? The World Trade Center..." But my mind wasn't focused on this conversation. I was thinking of my new grandson, Jonathan, born just three days earlier on the eighth.

As soon as I got home, I called my daughter in Tallahassee, Florida, to see how they were doing.

"Mom!" she exclaimed, "We've been trying to call you but couldn't get through! The World Trade Center..."

It was she who told me. I flipped on the TV as she spoke. However, only one channel was broadcasting because of what had been done to the towers. Finding that one, I, like most Americans, watched all day.

In my first reactions, I wondered, what other things were going to be blown up. Should I get out of New York City? And if so, what should I take with me? But where would be a safe place to go?

However, as days passed and I heard of military plans, increasing security at the airports, etc., I instinctively knew that security did not rely in these measures. Physically, no matter how much money was spent, there was no way that one could foreknow where to put policemen, scanners, and the military for certain safety. There could only be one antidote for fear—Security is in the Secret Place. Victory is only possible through weapons of the Spirit—love, joy peace, prayer, praise, faith, food, clothing, shelter, etc. If ever there was opportunity to learn this, it is now.

"911," people said, "The emergency number." However, God has a 911 number—Psalm 91:1: "*He that dwelleth in the Secret Place of the Most High shall abide under the shadow of the Almighty.*" This Psalm became an anchor for me: "*Thou shalt not be afraid of the terror... He shall give His angels charge over thee...*" I determined to be motivated by love and develop my inner listening powers.

from "Return to the Garden" in Somewhere on the Edge of Dreaming

"O divine Redeemer...Night gathers around my soul... Hear my cry... Come to me... Haste to help... In thy mercy, hear my cry..."

It has been my experience that when I cry, He comes. *"unto them who look for Him shall He appear."* When I am in despair and think I will never be happy again, *"Wait upon the Lord and He shall strengthen your heart."*

How many times have I been rescued? I can't count them. It may be in the form of an encouraging word, a phone call, a line from a book, a verse that leaps out at me or. . . a garden. ("God speaks in the guise of everything that happens," Martin Buber said.) "Amazing friends have been God's arms to hold and comfort me." I may be walking in nature, washing the dishes, taking a bath, or riding on the subway. Within my heart I hear a word. And I know I am not alone. I am loved. All is not lost.

And so I say, whatever the situation, "With divine help, I'm getting right back up and I'm going to walk in beauty. I will be steadfast in the steadfast love of God. I forgive and I am forgiven. *'No weapon formed against me will prosper... I dwell in the Secret Place of the Most High.'*"

"Faith is the evidence of things not seen." It takes time for faith to be perfected. Exercising the faith we do have, more and more we accept the mystical answers. Spirit beings temporarily in this temple, we learn not to *"judge by appearances"* but look beyond what our physical eyes and ears see and hear. In the energy of the flesh, we don't try to change externals to end conflict. We seek the whole picture and root causes. We ask for the wisdom we lack.

"Seeing Him, who is invisible," we walk and talk with Him in the Garden as a friend. We are at peace. *"...in quietness and confidence is our strength."* He is the One who says to the storm, *"Peace be still."*

Return to New York City? Return to the Garden.

September 3, 2010

I opened and these verses quickened: (from Isaiah 4-6)

"In that day shall the branch of the Lord be beautiful and glorious, and the fruit of the earth shall be excellent and comely... purged... by the spirit of judgment, and by the spirit of burning. And the Lord will create upon every dwelling place of mount Zion, and upon her assemblies, a cloud and smoke by day, and the shining of a flaming fire by night: for upon all the glory shall be a defense.

"And there shall be a tabernacle for a shadow in the daytime from the heat, and for a place of refuge, and for a covert from storm and from rain...

"And the mean man shall be brought down, and the mighty man shall be humbled, and the eyes of the lofty shall be humbled: But the Lord of hosts shall be exalted in judgment and God that is holy shall be sanctified in righteousness.

"Then shall the lambs feed after their manner, and the waste places of the fat ones shall strangers eat...

"Woe unto them that call evil good, and good evil: that put darkness for light, and light for darkness, that put bitter for sweet and sweet for bitter!

Woe unto them that are wise in their own eyes and prudent in their own sight! ...which justify the wicked for reward and take away the righteousness of the righteous from him!

"...And he will lift up an ensign to the nations from far...

"Therefore as the fire devoureth the stubble, and the flame consumeth the chaff, so their root shall be as rottenness and their blossom shall go up as dust because they have cast away the law of the Lord of hosts... [the Royal Law of Love-James]

"...I saw also the Lord sitting upon a throne, high and lifted up, and his train filled the temple. Above it stood the seraphim... and one cried unto another, and said, Holy, holy, holy, is the Lord of hosts: the whole earth is full of his glory...mine eyes have seen the King!"

Song:
I will sing of the mercies of the Lord forever,
  I will sing, I will sing.
I will sing of the mercies of the Lord forever,
  I will sing of the mercies of the Lord.

With my mouth will I make known
thy faithfulness, thy faithfulness,
With my mouth will I make known
thy faithfulness to all generations.

I will sing of the mercies of the Lord forever
I will sing of the mercies of the Lord.
--James Fillmore

"I will sing of the mercies of the Lord for ever: with my mouth will I make known thy faithfulness to all generations." (Psalm 89:1)

*The Brooklyn Bridge at Christmas time, with two of my eight
grandchildren
(Anabelle, seven and Patrick, eight).*

My son, Jack, is a structural engineer—designing
bridges—so naturally he is interested in bridges, and especially
the famous Brooklyn Bridge. He wanted his children to have
the experience of walking across it. Through the years I have
sent bridge postcards to him, and in so doing have thought of
a different kind of bridge—bridges of understanding between
people.

We can't build big bridges if we can't build small ones;
we can't have peace between nations if we can't have peace
between individuals.

www.ingramcontent.com/pod-product-compliance
Lightning Source LLC
Chambersburg PA
CBHW050546280326
41933CB00011B/1746